Taking the Driver's Seat

Living Life With Your Heart Fully Engaged

PATTY D. JOHNSON

Copyright © 2017 Patty D. Johnson

Taking the Driver's Seat
Living Life With Your Heart Fully Engaged

Published by Patty D. Johnson | Loudon, TN

Prepared for Publication by: www.palmtreeproductions.com

Printed in the USA

ISBN (print): 978-0-9989804-0-9

ISBN (Kindle): 978-0-9989804-1-6

Library of Congress Control Number: 2017906657

All Rights Reserved. This book is protected by the copyright laws of the United States of America. This book may not be copied or reprinted for commercial gain or profit. The use of short quotations is permitted. Permission will be granted upon request. The author guarantees all contents are original and do not infringe upon the legal rights of any other person or work.

Scripture references appear in the endnotes:

Scripture quotations marked (NIV) are taken from the HOLY BIBLE, NEW INTERNATIONAL VERSION®. Copyright © 1973, 1978, 1984 Biblica. Used by permission of Zondervan. All rights reserved.

Scripture quotations marked (NLT) are taken from the Holy Bible, New Living Translation. Copyright © 1996, 2004, 2007 by Tyndale House Foundation. Used by permission of Tyndale House Publishers, Inc., Carol Stream, Illinois 60188. All rights reserved.

Scripture quotations marked (TLB) are taken from The Living Bible copyright © 1971 by Tyndale House Foundation. Used by permission of Tyndale House Publishers Inc., Carol Stream, Illinois 60188. All rights reserved. The Living Bible, TLB, and the The Living Bible logo are registered trademarks of Tyndale House Publishers.

To Contact the Author:

www.pattydjohnson.com

Dedication

To the Women and Men of Aglow International

It is such a blessing and joy in my life to be an Aglow woman. I count it an honor to be numbered in their ranks. Over and over and over, my Aglow sisters have been there for me. In our worldwide family of Aglow, our friendships are eternal. We have shared car trips together, bus trips, plane trips, boat trips, hotel rooms, beds, bathrooms, snacks, pillows and hair products. Together we have generously undergirded the restaurant business across this great nation from one end to the other. We have prayed together in our national capitols, in our state capitols, in airports, on the streets, in rehabilitation centers and again and again and again in the land of Israel. We love and trust one another and we build together shoulder to shoulder.

Aglow International, you have given me love and affirmation. We have celebrated together and cried together. You have given me role models of authentic, Spirit-led leadership. You have given me open doors of opportunity to serve and influence. You have provided world-class mentoring, extravagant worship experiences and consistent prophetic impartation. You have given me a place to stand ... a place in which to lift up my voice for the King. With all my heart, I thank you. We will walk together till He comes!

To Graham Cooke

For many years, Graham has been a faithful friend, passionate comrade, mentor, teacher and prophetic voice to Aglow International. I have been richly mentored and transformed through his writings and personally trained under his Game Changers material. In his own words, Graham Cooke's ministry is marked by his delightful, intimate, and unreserved two-way friendship with the Lord. The radiant truths he has imparted to me undergird every page of my book.

What Others Are Saying

Sharing with authentic transparency, Patty Johnson gives you a front row seat in her own journey towards becoming fully who God created her to be. You will smile, and maybe shed a tear or two, as you will relate easily to her life experiences. You will also glean from the insights and truths Patty draws from her very personal process of "becoming." A great book to not only read, but pass on to a friend or loved one who needs a message of hope and encouragement.

— Jane Hansen Hoyt
President/CEO, Aglow International

Patty Johnson is a dear friend, a minister of the gospel and full of bold tenacity to strengthen, encourage and empower others to take the position of being in the driver's seat of their lives. In *Taking the Driver's Seat* of her own life, Patty boldly spoke to the mountain before her as in Matthew 21:21, *"Be thou removed and cast into the midst of the sea."* In her book, Patty reveals the sufferings of the victim mentality and replaces that mentality with a love from her heavenly Father. This transition has moved her to a place of victory and a mindset of unlimited possibilities, truths, and ultimately, breakthrough. She took back her identity and her dignity and so can you. I believe this book can and will empower you to walk in confidence, security and with stability in your daily walk with Christ.

—Lynda (Coleman) Dicandio
Senior Pastor New Hope Assembly of God, Tellico Plains, Tennessee

Everyone wants to fly and soar above the circumstances of their lives. Get ready to take flight above your circumstances as you read this book. Patty's story is a living example of God's incredible grace and God's unending love. Despite your brokenness, God wants to take you higher than you ever imagined. You are God's creation and He has an amazing plan for you. Just as Patty did, as you embrace your identity in Christ, you will begin to mount up with wings like eagles. You can fly.

—**Terry G. Bailey**
District Superintendent, Tennessee Assemblies of God Ministry Network

All people long to be all they can be, yet most are content to live on the sidelines and watch others play the game of life. In Patty's book, *Taking the Driver's Seat,* long lost dreams will be restored as each reader realizes that tough times, as well as "mistakes," do not disqualify them from a journey filled with freedom and fullness. The truths that unfold are destined to bring many out of darkness into a glorious place of freedom. I am sure that this book will be a best seller as it should be given to those in our sphere of influence who do not see themselves as God sees them. I see a mighty army rising up as they read through the pages of this empowering book.

—**Kathy Sanders**
Executive Director of Leader Development, Aglow International

Being comfortable in your own skin and living confidently with boldness is no small thing. In *Taking the Driver's Seat,* Patty inspires you to live free, regardless of what has held you bound. When you read this book, you will see yourself through God's eyes and learn how to wait in adversity and trust Him in all things.

—**Wendy K. Walters**
Motivational Speaker, Founder of The Favor Foundation

Prologue	ix
Introduction	1

PART ONE
Conquering Defeat
5

Chapter One — 7
Flying on The Titanic

Chapter Two — 17
Taking Back Your Identity

PART TWO
Activating Your Uniqueness
45

Chapter Three — 47
Enlisting for The Plan

Chapter Four — 75
Letting Your Heart Come Forward

PART THREE
Taking The Driver's Seat
105

Chapter Five — 107
Living in Confident Boldness

Chapter Six — 129
Setting the Banquet Table

Meet the Author — 151

Prologue

the JOY OF HEAVEN

It was early January when my pastor asked me if I would preach the Sunday message later that month. In the year previous to that, I had shared on an assortment of topics that were all significant to me. Yet now, as I prayed and sought the Lord in the days that followed, something felt different. I could sense a rumbling in my spirit that something was up, and I knew clearly that this time the Lord was asking me to share my personal testimony.

Sharing my story was not at all new for me. I had shared it many times as a speaker in other venues. But even though I was only weeks away from being ordained, I had never shared my testimony in church. In fact, I had never considered it. The whole thing took me by surprise and felt very out of the blue. I did not understand yet that the Lord was transitioning me into a new season, and that something was being intentionally shifted over my life.

So sure enough, that is the message I brought that morning, and sure enough, the joy of Heaven broke forth. I found myself watching people's faces lighting up all over the room as they experienced the love of God reaching out and embracing them. There was a very real and tangible joy from heaven loosed in our midst. It was convincingly evident to me that the Holy Spirit was breathing upon this story of my life journey with all of its twists and turns of rejection, shame and torment. The story had been laid aside for a long time, but it was now about to become the core message of my life.

During this very same period of time, I had been experiencing a growing desire in my heart to write a new book. I kept wanting, and trying, to give myself to the task, but there was a fogginess surrounding it. Nothing felt right, and I could not seem to move forward. It did not happen overnight, but there was a very real moment of revelation when suddenly I connected the common thread. **God wanted me to share my story.** He wanted me to share the broken pieces of my life ... the testimony of His grace and love for a woman who, by the world's standards, would have been a statistical failure, but for whom He had another plan. He wanted it told so that other lives could be spared through the same impartation of His healing and restoration.

> "Joy is the serious business of heaven."
>
> —C.S. Lewis

Introduction

WHO IS *driving*?

I love to dream. God really speaks to me in dreams. However, it was quite a long time before I actually got this whole thing about cars and being in the driver's seat. For years I would have dreams where I was in a car, but it was always someone else's car. In my dreams, they would be driving and I would be a passenger. Usually, I would be sitting in the back seat. Six years ago, I actually made it into my own car! I should have baked cupcakes and thrown a party that day. But here is the deal. Yes, it was my car … but I was not in the driver's seat!

Thankfully, I did not know how many years and how many dreams it would take until I actually got into my own driver's seat. I have had multiple dreams about my car. Each one is a story in itself. In all those dreams, I either could not find my car, I was sitting in the passenger side of my car waiting for the driver to come, or I was in my car while someone else was driving it. Hmmm ... that can be quite revealing! Recently, I had my first dream where I was in my car, and I was in the driver's seat. That got my attention. It was probably another occasion when we should have had cupcakes. Since then, I have had some really awesome adventures in my dreams while driving my own car.

We are going to talk about all this in this book. Who is driving your car? If you were to have a dream tonight with your car in it, would you be in the driver's seat? If your answer is no, do you know who *would* be in the driver's seat? For many of you, God wants to promote you into the driver's seat of your life. All that really means is that you have passed your tests, and you have become more than a conqueror of your wilderness experiences. Your mindset has been transformed and renewed, and you now have enough love that the Lord can trust you with the keys to the life that He longs for you to have.

For most of you who picked up this book, and have hopefully purchased it, you know something is not right. You can feel it. That is why words like *driver's seat* and *your heart fully engaged* called out your name. You know that life is meant to be more than what you are experiencing. For some of you, it has been this way for a long time. *Taking the Driver's Seat* is not a book about usurping anyone else's place in life. It is not a book about demanding your rights. This book is about your becoming so deeply secure in your Father's goodness, and so deeply secure in His affirmation and celebration of who you are, that people and circumstances no longer consign you to an emotional roller coaster. It is about knowing, boldly and confidently and unapologetically, the place that is yours to occupy in God and standing up on the inside of yourself and occupying that place. The title of this book and the purpose of this book all have to do with your replacing a victim mindset of defeat with a victory mindset of unlimited possibilities.

Scattered throughout the chapters, you are going to find pieces of my own personal story. As you read these stories and interact with the reflections following each chapter, either on your own or as part of a discussion group, you are going to have an encounter with truth. This truth is going to empower you to break through very real lies of darkness that have captured your heart. You are going to begin to connect with those things that are stealing your freedom, and you will be equipped with truth to disempower them.

The expertise that I bring to the table is that I have lived these things and now I am free. God brought me through to freedom, and He is going to bring you through too. You will recognize yourself in my stories. You will relate to the lies that I believed about myself … lies that misrepresented the Father's true character and which therefore prolonged my healing. You will read about destructive emotions that I wrestled with and behaviors that tormented me. You are also going to read about my victories, and when you do, it is going to resonate deep within your own spirit.

The pure, innocent and beautiful child that lives in you, the child in you who wants desperately to find your way home to the Father's arms of love, is going to giggle out loud. There may even be tears ... because you have been fighting an unseen enemy for a long time, and you are weary. There is a fight that is screaming inside you, "There is more! There is more! I know there is more!" You are going to learn a new language of hope for your future, and that new language is going to close the door to your past and release your heart to take flight once again.

Are you ready?
Fasten your seat belt!

Part One

CONQUERING DEFEAT

But in all these things we overwhelmingly conquer through Him who loved us.
—ROMANS 8:37, NASB

Chapter One

Flying on The Titanic

the DREAM

I dreamed a dream. I dreamed I was on the great Titanic and I was flying. I was flying everywhere all over the magnificent ship. I would zoom with crazy speed through the long, inner corridors and up and down the grand, winding staircases. I flew down into the dark, lower level of the ship, and I spoke to people down there that I knew. Then I zoomed up several staircases until I was on the very highest deck of the ship. I was flying all around everywhere as passengers were mingling about. The sky was brilliant blue, the sun was shining, and it was exhilarating! The passengers were all captivated as they were excitedly watching me, and they all wanted to learn how to do it. So I came down into an open, grassy area on the deck where I could teach them, and they all gathered around me.

As I stood there on the grass, I tried to take flight. I just kept trying over and over to make my legs lift off, but it would not work. All at once, I knew that I needed to find higher ground. I looked around and saw a stone wall of some sort that wrapped around a nearby swimming pool. It was only about two feet high, so I easily climbed up and stood on it, and from there it was easy to take off. As I flew, I laughed joyfully, and announced to everyone, "The secret is you have to take off from a high place!"

As I continued flying, I became aware that I was wearing a heavy, cumbersome winter coat. I was having the time of my life flying, but I knew that I would be able to fly better without the coat. So I took the coat off. I just boldly took it off. When I did, I laughed out loud again ... I discovered that I was flying in a bikini! Then the dream ended.

I love dreams. Don't you? When Jesus talked to people about Heaven and about His Father, He told a lot of stories, and He would often speak in parables. I believe when He gives us a dream, it is a lot like a parable. He has a sense of humor and He knows that dreams can be fun. He likes to hide spiritual treasures inside our night dreams to see if we will actually go hunting for them, and He has tucked a lot of spiritual treasures inside this dream.[1]

HIDDEN TREASURES

The very first spiritual treasure we encounter in my dream is the attraction of the human heart to the euphoria of being airborne. We all agree that flying feels magical; it puts a smile on our face. All over the world, little children play the same game, running and running at full speed, flailing their arms, purring like an engine gearing up and then finally imagining they are lifting off in full flight. Oh, how intoxicating is the exhilaration of perceived flight! Generation after generation has fallen in love with Walt Disney's classic Peter Pan movies. And all ages are captivated by the short-tempered Tinker Bell, his 1953 adaptation of the little fairy with her magical pixie dust. The golden, glitter-like powder came from Tinker Bell's wings and granted the abilities of flight to all those who thought happy thoughts.

> *The moment you doubt whether you can fly, you cease for ever to be able to do it.*
> — J.M. BARRIE, *PETER PAN*

Everything in my dream is about the nuances of mastering the art of flying. Flying represents the heart's personal freedom, and the second spiritual treasure that we encounter in the dream is that flying represents a heart that is not tethered to the people or events surrounding it. It represents a heart that has learned how to live from a place above the surrounding circumstances. Not every day is going to be an ideal day for our heart to take flight. Family relationships alone can dictate stormy weather conditions and prevailing winds that would withstand flight. Yet when our heart has truly mastered flying, it has learned how to live gracefully with those companions who are onboard the great ship of life with us. It has learned how to love them even when they have not yet experienced the freedom that we have ... and even when they have no desire to leave the dark, lower level where we too once lived.

> **Our heart flies when we are free!**

We know how to love them in that place, but we do not hang our hat there, or more significantly, we do not hang our heart there. We have trained ourselves to know how to rise up, up, up to the high places. We have submitted ourselves to a painful, rigorous process of transformation by the renewing of our mind,[2] and you will now find us hanging out on the upper deck, our soul warmed by the sun and refreshed by the soft ocean breeze. That is what it means to fly.

The third spiritual treasure that we encounter in the dream is the secret to flying. There is a secret to flying, and others are attracted to people who have learned the secret. "The secret is you have to take off from a high place!" The high place is the antithesis of the low place. Your heart can never take flight from a place of bitterness. You must come up higher and exchange your bitterness for forgiveness. Your heart can never take flight from a place of defeat. You must come up higher and exchange your defeat for hope. Your heart can never take flight from a place of unbelief.[3] You must come up higher and exchange your unbelief for faith.

There are lies that have set up housekeeping within our heart. Our heart will simply not ever become unstuck from those lies until we intentionally displace the lies with truth. Should you choose not to do so, the soles of your shoes will refuse to release you from that low ground, and you will stay there and petrify into stone. Flight will never overtake you. God wants to take you to higher ground. He wants to award you your flight instructor's license. There are many in line behind you, and in days ahead, you will be teaching them.

Finally, the fourth spiritual treasure that we encounter in the dream is that flying represents a heart that is totally abandoned to boldly embracing its own uniqueness. It cares not if no one else in the room is flying. It has learned long ago how to be happy enough to fly solo when needed. This entire focus of confident, personal freedom is sharply portrayed

> **Our heart flies when we boldly embrace our uniqueness!**

through the spontaneous shedding of the heavy, winter coat.

As we journey through life, we accumulate all sorts of outer garments that serve to protect us from being fully known, even to ourselves. These garments will need to be removed in order to facilitate ease of flight and to accommodate promotion to higher levels. In contrast to the weighted coat, the surprise bikini portrays a light-hearted abandonment and a transparency that permits others to see more of the real you. It speaks of an absence of self-consciousness and self-awareness and of an agenda that has nothing to hide. It represents the substance of child-like innocence.

the INVITATION

Your Father has a dream for your life. He wants you to fly. The Titanic was a great, magnificent ship. It was opulent and extravagant. It was a wealthy ocean vessel. The Titanic is a fitting picture of the place of abundance and fulfillment that the Lord dreams of for you. Nothing that you have done, or that others have done to you, can nullify the largeness of the dream that the Father in Heaven dreams over your life. He dreams for you that your heart will fly.

The purpose of this chapter has been to awaken the child-like wonder within your heart to believe again. Do you remember the above quote from Peter Pan, "The moment you doubt whether you can fly, you cease for ever to be able to do it"? Today the Lord is inviting you to let go of all doubt. He is asking you to believe. As you process through the chapters of this book, the Lord desires to do an overhaul of the foundation upon which your life is presently built. Your old foundation is going to be dismantled, and a new foundation is going to be dug down deep and laid on rock. *I will show you what he is like who comes to me and hears my words and puts them into practice. He is like a man building a house, who dug down deep and laid the foundation on rock. When a flood came, the torrent struck that house but could not shake it, because it was well built.*[4]

Once your life is well built upon the right foundation, the flood torrents may strike you, but they will no longer be strong enough to effectively shake you. This rock that the foundation of your life must be laid upon is the Father's love, and it must be laid deep. It must become an unshakable, living certainty and reality in the very core of your being that you are loved by all of Heaven. The Lord's love for you must become a non-negotiable conviction that governs all your life. "I am a child of God and I am loved by my Father!" must become your battle cry, for it is His love that will empower you to stand up on the inside. It is the ultimate high place, the pinnacle, from which you will always take flight.

CONCLUSION

God is inviting you to take flight. Flying is an expression of joy, and the joy of the Lord is your strength. He knows you are surrounded by difficult circumstances and by people who do not know about flying. He wants you to stay connected to these people. But when they cannot join you, He wants you to fly anyway. He has new truth for you, and you are going to be surprised at how spontaneously you will begin to just throw off some old mindsets simply because you no longer want to be weighed down by them. You are going to step into a new confidence and a child-like freedom and transparency that are going to make room for the real you to come forth.

These things do not have to take years. Your breakthrough is going to come quickly

PRAYER

Father, thank You. I accept Your invitation. Lord, I choose to begin this journey with You, and I know that You are holding my hand as we go. Awaken my heart to Your love that I might learn to fly in the high places above my circumstances. Wash away the pain and the tears and the disappointments, Lord, and make me strong in You. I love You. Amen

THOUGHTS *for* REFLECTION *and* DISCUSSION

1. Close your eyes and imagine yourself in this dream. Take time to really see it.
   - What are you feeling as you zoom about?
   - When you fly down into the dark, lower level of the ship, who do you see down there?
   - Are you excited about teaching the other passengers how to fly?
   - Do you feel self-conscious about removing your heavy winter coat?
   - What about the bikini? Are you able to grasp the spiritual truth that the Holy Spirit is portraying through the bikini?
   - If you do not dream, and you want to dream, begin asking the Holy Spirit to give you dreams while you sleep. Job 33:14-15
2. Which spiritual truth(s) spoke to you? In what way?
3. What would flying above your circumstances look like for you?
4. Write out what you are feeling whenever you try to connect with your heart.

5. Describe what was happening the last time that you experienced Jesus' love for you.

Endnotes
1. Proverbs 8:17 NIV.
2. Romans 12:2 NIV.
3. Proverbs 4:23 NIV.
4. Luke 6:48 NIV

---

*"What if I fall?"
Oh, but my darling, what if you fly?*

—Erin Hanson

Chapter Two

Taking Back Your Identity

PART ONE—TESTIMONY

WHEN the FAMILY FAILS Inspection

We sat in a conference room around a large table. There were eight teachers, the school principal, and myself. As the meeting came to a close, the principal spoke with great concern. "Mrs. Johnson, unless something drastic should happen, both your sons will end up spending time in prison." They were twelve years old.

It had been only a few months earlier, as the school year was just beginning, that the principal had sought me out at the open house for parents. His words that night had been like honey to a mother's heart, and when I went home, I wrote them in my journal: *So you are Eric and Danny's mother. What a pleasure it is to meet you. I am so delighted to have your boys with us. I have never seen two students who carried a greater potential for leadership. Why, if your boys announced they were selling tickets to the moon, every student in this school would be in line tomorrow to buy one!*

How quickly the honey had turned bitter. And the trip to the moon had been cancelled. It was difficult seeing through the tears as I drove home from that late afternoon conference. Storm clouds gathered in my heart, and out loud I began to sing the song that was destined to carry me for many years to come:

> *Thou, O Lord, art a shield about me.*
> *You're my glory and the lifter up of my head.*[1]

That seventh grade year Eric and Danny accumulated more than two hundred detentions. Each detention was accompanied by a personal phone call from the school office and a notice sent home to be signed. Together they were suspended fifty-two days. Their report cards came home with straight F's. In the early spring they were both expelled, and they failed the school year. The following year, convinced that all would be well, I home schooled them. Then, our hopes high, we enrolled them in an all-boys' school. But in only a few short months they were expelled.

At the time, our two daughters were attending a private Christian school in which we were very involved, and the men serving on the board of regents were our friends. But the school was unwilling to accept our sons for enrollment. We found a smaller Christian school forty-five minutes from our home that was willing to take them. For several months I drove the round-trip twice a day, taking them in the morning and picking them up in the afternoon. I was driving three hours a day to keep them in school. After four months they were again expelled.

They began smoking and were beginning to have incidents with alcohol. For years they had been excellent athletes. In their younger years, their father had always been one of their coaches, and their games were a bright and happy part of our life. But now they began to be dismissed from their athletic teams. They were dismissed from youth group and from Sunday school and were no longer permitted to attend. During all this, my husband Hollis was promoted to a new position at work, and we relocated to a new city and a new school district. It seemed like a ray of hope and a new beginning, as we had literally run out of schools. But it was only a very short time until they were expelled once more and were back at home with no school options.

Our life began to unravel at an alarmingly rapid pace. Neither of our sons could hold down a job and were fired repeatedly. They were fifteen now and would often be gone from home for days at a time. Every night we would bolt and lock down our car to prevent them from taking it. They began to be involved with crime and with the legal system, and for years there was a continuous presence of police cars in our driveway.

> **Our life began to unravel at an alarmingly rapid pace**

My life became consumed with driving them to ever-changing jobs, often long distances away, and often night factory hours. I drove them to court hearings, to meetings with probation officers, to work-crew restitution, and to AA meetings. There was an endless parade of long, mandatory, court-ordered meetings that we as parents were required to attend. For a long time I was naïve about their drug usage and about the seriousness of their growing addiction. They became increasingly angry and violent. There was continual lying and insidious, chilling, demonic laughter. There was disrespect, mockery, belligerence, and cursing. There was broken furniture and blood and punctured holes in the drywall. There were threatening and harassing phone calls from drug dealers at all hours of the night. For years we slept with our wallets. More than once, they forged large checks which then caused our bank account to bounce. They sold their clothing and many precious gifts that we had given them in order to pay for their drugs.

The storm did not last for just a season, nor was it only for a time. It did not end and it did not get better. It only continued to grow darker and darker. We wanted to make it stop, but nothing we did brought any change. My parents disowned me and would no longer come to our home. Both sides of our family wrote hateful, condemning letters to us telling us that we had failed as parents and were fully to blame. I remember once coming home with groceries, pulling our car into the garage, and starting into the house. Suddenly, I collapsed onto the garage floor, laid my head on the cold cement step, and began to sob and sob and sob. "Oh God," I cried, "I can't go in. I can't do it anymore." Our home had become a prison.

Danny's drug usage became alarming. His speech became slurred and he was no longer able to track or follow conversation. Both he and Eric were admitted into the local hospital for several weeks, but they began using again as soon as they were discharged. I became panicky and would often cling to Hollis to make it through the night. I was unstable and I felt desperate.

I called Danny's aftercare drug counselor and asked permission to bring Danny in again. I sat in the waiting area of the hospital while they met together. After a long time, his counselor's door opened, and Danny came out first. He was swaggering and laughing, and his eyes seemed hollow and far away as he came toward me. "Oh Mom," he said, "I'm gonna be dead before I'm twenty one. Just like Jimmy Morrison, Mom." I jumped out of my chair. I ran to Danny, took him in my arms, and screamed at the top of my voice, "No! No! It's a lie from hell! You will live! And you will serve God!" I held onto him and kissed and kissed his neck. "I love you, Danny! I love you!" He was sixteen and more than six feet tall. He took hold of me, and his tears ran down my neck, wetting my shirt, as he pleaded desperately, "Please help me, Mom. Please help me. I'm so sick."

The week following Christmas we admitted Danny to a long-term treatment facility located three hours from our home. He would live there for the next several months. During his stay we made the three-hour trip twice a week for family group therapy and then again every Sunday for visiting. In time, Eric was asked not to come, as he was smuggling in drugs and cigarettes to Danny. It was an emotionally exhausting seven months during which we put almost twenty-five thousand miles on our car. Our hearts were filled with hope when at long last we packed up his things and brought him home. We celebrated and released a carload of helium balloons. On the first weekend back Danny began using again.

There were too many felonies to keep count. There were police officers in my yard, my kitchen, my basement and my bedrooms. There were sirens, guns, search warrants, handcuffs, shackles, electronic beepers, and courtroom after courtroom. The judges soon knew us and suggested that perhaps a wing of the building ought to be named after us. Over time we visited our sons in thirteen separate prisons, some far away, and we often left home in the darkness of night to arrive on time for visitation hours.

Emotional ROBBERY

Is there a moment when daylight ends and night begins? Or do the rays of light go out one by one until the spirit of man is broken? My life had grown very dark ... a darkness so thick I could feel it ... a darkness so cold that I was frightened. Can the night last too long? Years and years and years ... sobbing ... shaking ... screaming ... pounding the walls until my arms were black and blue. Thrashing through the night. Afraid. Always so afraid. Deep darkness. Desperation. Fear and torment.

CHOOSE *life*

Winter ended, summer came, and soon they would be coming home from prison. They were eighteen years old now, and in my heart I still dreamed of their high-school graduation. One night very late, while Hollis slept, I got up out of bed, put on shorts and a t-shirt, and drove to the high-school baseball field. I parked the car and walked out onto the field. The moon was shining full and bright as I walked the bases. I walked them a second time. Then I stopped at home plate and stood there remembering. In my heart, I could see them as little boys. I could still see the crisp, red and white uniforms, and I could see them through all the years and all the games. I could see their muscular arms, tan and lean, poised in the air as they stood waiting for the pitch. I could hear the crack of the bat and remember all those times I had shot up out of the bleachers, erupting into shouts of joy as they slid into home plate.

Years of emotions erupted. This time I ran the bases. Then slowly, blinded by tears, I walked out and stood on the pitcher's mound. I remembered the game when Danny had struck out eighteen batters in a row. My heart broke, and I cried out to heaven, "O Lord, please! Please! Let them play baseball again. Let the sun shine again, Lord!" Then I fell on the mound and wept and wept and wept.

That week I was admitted to the hospital and diagnosed with Crohn's disease. I spent three weeks in bed and lost over twenty pounds. I was not able to make the trip with Hollis to pick Eric and Danny up, but they were home only a few days when I knew. I knew they would not be returning to high school. I knew there would be no senior pictures and no senior prom. And I knew there would be no more baseball games. I wrote in my journal:

For you, O God, tested us; you refined us like silver. You brought us into prison and laid burdens on our backs. You let men ride over our heads; we went through fire and water, but you brought us to a place of abundance.[2]

But You brought us into the place of abundance ... How famished my soul was for the place of abundance! O Lord, my God, how long ... how long? Days passed, and once more I wrote words in my journal:

I am not sure what all God had purposed in this, but I find myself left with no life, very tired, believing that my work is done. I have a strong desire to go home. The ongoing burden of life leaves me numb. Things are so hard. I just want peace. I feel great love toward the Lord because I know He would not do anything toward me except out of His love to perfect me. I just feel very tired and so aware that life is only pain followed by more pain. Whereas I once desired to be conformed to His image, now I just want release. There was no reward for any of our labor. I long deeply to go home. I see the Father on a porch sitting in a rocker. I want Him to hold me on His lap and rock me and rock me and whisper in my ear, "You did good, Patty. You did good."

> **I once desired to be conformed to His image, now I just want release**

I began to pray that the Lord would come and take me. On the second night, I fell asleep praying that. In the middle of that night, I was awakened from a sound sleep as I felt His Presence in the room. I sat upright in my bed, listening, and in my heart I clearly heard Him speak these words, "This day I have set before you life and death. Now choose life, Patty, so that you and your children may live."³

*The cords of death entangled me; the torrents of destruction overwhelmed me. The cords of the grave coiled around me; the snares of death confronted me. He reached down from on high and took hold of me; he drew me out of deep waters. He rescued me from my powerful enemy, from my foes, who were too strong for me.*⁴ Death. Destruction. The grave. Cords and torrents and snares. Entangled and overwhelmed. But that night Jesus reached down, took hold of me, and rescued me. He breathed His resurrection life and power into me and raised me up from the dead. And even as the storm raged on, there grew within the inner sanctuary of my heart a place of refuge and fortification where fear could no longer penetrate.

CHOOSE *life* AGAIN

Eric and Danny continued to be tossed to and fro. In a few months we made them move out because of their violent tempers, drug addiction, and disrespect. Their lives were chaotic and without direction, and Danny was soon incarcerated again. The following summer we rented a cabin up north and invited Eric to come. We were not aware that he was dating, but he brought a young girl with him whom we had never met. One sunny afternoon I grabbed a book and curled up on the sofa that faced out over the lake. I had been reading a long time when the cabin door opened, and I looked up to see Angie. As she came through the door and into the cabin, the rays of the late afternoon sun caught her silhouette from behind, and I instantly realized that she was pregnant. She was carrying our first grandchild.

Only a few weeks later, after we were at home again, I came in from the mailbox carrying a letter from Danny. I opened his letter and read the words he had written from prison: *I guess you know Jessica is pregnant with my baby.* Angie was pregnant. Jessica was pregnant. There were two babies on the way. Jessica and Angie had been best friends since kindergarten. They would be entering ninth grade in the fall, and both babies were due in only a few months. Conflict and turmoil rolled inside me like waves of the sea as I saw my future crumbling before me. I had not known how tenaciously I was still holding on to my own dreams for Eric and Danny. The foundation beneath my feet was cracking, and deeply entrenched roots within my battered heart were gasping for air.

Early Monday morning, I did what I had done for years on Monday mornings. I got into my car and drove out the long country road to my friend's beautiful farmhouse. Week after week, year after year, Mary and I had met there around her kitchen table to worship and pray. We would share our hearts and talk about our families. We would pray for the church and for the nations. We would laugh and cry together and sometimes shout and dance. That morning as I sat there with her, I knew what needed to be done. I knew I had to lay it down ... all of it. I knew I had to let go and entrust it all into God's hand, but a force as strong as iron was resisting me. My heart felt plundered and violated, and the hill in front of me felt too steep to climb. I screamed out in agony as the dream inside me resisted its death. Then quietly, with Mary's love making a way, I bowed my head and prayed through tears, "Lord Jesus, I receive the babies. Lord, I thank you for sending them into our lives. Lord Jesus, I receive these little angels and all that they have for us." The dam broke and His peace flooded my heart.

Emily and Mandy were born six weeks apart. They stole their way into our hearts, and we helped in every way we could. Their daddies drifted in and out, and their relationships with Angie and Jessica became turbulent. One summer evening we were keeping Mandy for the night. She was just a little toddler. She loved her daddy, and her eyes lit all up that night when he unexpectedly came by. For a short time they played together. But then, with no good-byes, Danny disappeared out through the back garage door and was off and gone to his own world.

Mandy wandered through every room looking for him. Her tiny legs climbed the stairs one at a time, searching every upstairs room for him and calling his name. I could not stop her. Finally, abandoned and betrayed, her little heart burst, her lips quivered, and through broken sobs the words tumbled out, "Wh ... wh ... where Daddy g ... g ... go? Wh ... wh ... where Daddy g ... g ... go, Gramma?"

My own tears burst forth as the stinking, rotten pain and anguish of it all washed over me. I collapsed onto the floor, drawing Mandy into my lap, longing to shield her and yet knowing I never could. Back and forth, back and forth, we rocked as I joined the wail of heaven.

They were part of our life for many years. We chased rainbows together, caught fireflies, built sand castles, and filled photograph albums. We ate ice-cream together at the county fair and blew out birthday candles with each other. Time passed, and the families felt it best to sever ties with us. And as quickly as they had come into our lives, just as quickly they were gone.

I do not believe that I understood during that time the deep work that the Lord was doing in my heart. There were profound, profound changes taking place within me, and I would never be the same. In that same season, our youngest daughter moved home from Colorado with her little newborn son. She was alone and needed help. He was just days older than our daughter Melissa's new baby. My life and home were suddenly filled with babies, and deep wells of love were being uncapped within me. The old familiar landscape of my heart was fading away, and tiny new seedlings were being quietly planted by the Gardener. It would be years before they matured, but I could feel the faint stirrings of new life. So many times during those years, Jesus and I would just sit together quietly, just being with each other, as I struggled to embrace the new place, and to even lay aside personal dreams for my own life. In those times I would sing to Him out of my overwhelming love for all that He was to me, and He would give me words to heal the loneliness.

PART TWO—INSIGHTS

the BELIEVER'S TRUE IDENTITY

I titled this chapter, "Taking Back Your Identity." The reason you need to take something back is because it has been stolen from you. Your identity equates to your being in the driver's seat of your life. You need to take back whatever it is that you lost that has caused you to be repositioned into the passenger's seat of life or, worse yet, the back seat. Your identity has been confiscated. Confiscation is defined as the seizure of private property. Therefore, the term identity confiscation refers to the seizure of an individual's identity. The enemy's confiscation of an individual believer's identity is the most effective tactical weapon in his arsenal, because loss of identity renders a believer powerless. Knowing and operating in your identity is what puts you in the driver's seat of your life, and knowing and operating in your identity is what keeps you in the driver's seat of your life. Surrendering your identity in any way, even through ignorance, will remove you from that seat.

So what exactly is a believer's identity? Identity encompasses the sum total of all that defines an individual believer's inherent uniqueness as a child of God. It embraces every distinction and nuance that our Heavenly Father poured into a particular life when He fashioned and created it. It includes every dream that the Father, Son and Holy Spirit dreamed for you when They sat around the table together before the creation of the world, having a morning coffee, and excitedly discussing you. It includes your *knowing that you came from God and that you will return to God*.[5] It includes your knowing that *before He formed you in the womb He knew you*.[6] The Father's thoughts and purposes for you were decided upon in advance when He intently fashioned you to be a distinctly original reflection of Himself. Your confident ownership and demonstration of that identity is what the enemy seeks to steal from you.

> *"Every single one of you has an identity that Heaven knows and understands. You are known in Heaven. When you receive a prophetic word, what's happening? God is saying, 'This is how We see you. This is how We view you. This is what We believe you are about.'"*
>
> —GRAHAM COOKE

Each of us has identity distinctions that are common to all believers and identity distinctions that are very personally ours according to our calling and destiny. For the purpose of this discussion, we are not distinguishing between the two. It is imperative that you know your identity as God's child, and it is imperative that you keep your identity throughout every battle you engage in. Know foremost that the enemy's intention is always to negate or dilute the identity that was given to you by your Father. You are fearfully and wonderfully made in accordance with the eternal purpose of your Father. You come forth from the womb perfectly wired to enjoy and prosper in all your assignments, and, throughout all your days, you walk under the smile of an open heaven. This is the core of your identity. You really are meant to fly.

In the natural world that we live in, carrying proof of our identity is everyday basic equipment. We cannot board an airplane, legally drive a car, retrieve a small child from daycare or cash a check without proper personal identification. The natural world has natural barricades in place that cannot be passed through without proper identification. This same principle is paralleled in the spiritual realm. As long as we are secure in our identity, as long as we have our heart wrapped around the Father's unshakable commitment to us, we can proceed and overcome through all obstacles. But at whatever point we permit our spiritual identity to be confiscated and stripped from us, at whatever point we allow ourselves to believe that the Lord's hand has let go of ours, at that point we become blocked, and we are powerless to victoriously navigate through the daily warfare of life. The barricades erected in the spiritual realm will not yield passage to us, and we are stymied.

Again, refusing to relinquish your spiritual identity, keeping your identity intact through every battle, is the DNA of taking the driver's seat. Taking the driver's seat of your life is an act of worship. It is a personal act of worship wherein you make a choice to stand up on the inside of yourself and own your identity as your Father's much loved child. A child of God who is secure in that identity can be surrounded by outright chaos and at the same time be at peace. Satan will come to contest and abort the fail-proof plan that was determined, established and finalized over your life in the heavenly dialogue that took place long ago around that table. But you are the object of His love, and as long as you stay planted in that identity, God will be faithful to cause all your circumstances to work together for good. In everything, He is growing you up in love.

an ORPHAN SPIRIT

Whenever we are persevering through a prolonged season in the wilderness, identity confiscation can often become the end result. The trials of our journey can wound our soul. Our heart, once bright with hope, recedes and withdraws, until we no longer have the strength to feel. I wrote in my journal: *But I found myself left with no life, very tired, eventually believing that my work was done, and finally a strong desire to go home. The ongoing burden of life left me numb. Things were so hard. I just wanted peace.* We can come to a place where we long for release. We are present in a situation, and suddenly we don't want to be present anymore.

When our spiritual identity becomes compromised, the vacant space will always be replaced with a false identity. This false identity is a lie. The lie will then cause us to begin to see our circumstances through a darkened lens. One of the lies that we can easily fall victim to is referred to as an orphan spirit. The word orphan, in its basic form, refers to a child who has been deprived by death of one, or usually both, parents. However, the word is also used to imply a child who has been deprived of some protection or advantage … a child who has been robbed of something needed, wanted or expected, especially a nonmaterial asset.

An orphan spirit will manifest itself as an overwhelming sense of abandonment. An orphan spirit will cause you to strike out in accusation against the goodness of God's heart and character. You feel that God has not been there for you. He did not protect you. He did not answer your prayers. You feel abandoned and alone in your pain, because He did not do what you needed Him to do. Because you feel uncared for, your heart now allows the enemy to malign the Father's true identity to you. When this happens, you have surely lost your way and stand in need of being found. That is when the Father leaves the ninety-nine in the open country and comes after you until He finds you. Then in His love *He joyfully puts you on His shoulders and takes you home.*[7]

> *"When wanting to cast out an orphan heart, remember that you can displace it only by introducing it to a loving Father."*
>
> —JACK FROST, PASTOR

the FATHER'S TRUE IDENTITY

Our Heavenly Father is a loving Father. Any other image of His Fatherhood is a distorted image. We must never attribute the work of Satan to the Father. Your Father is not the author of pain. He does not inflict you with drug addiction. He does not cause the breakdown of your family relationships in order to mature you. He does not keep you in bondage to shame, torment and fear out of a desire to perfect you. He does not cause you to hate and reject yourself. Physical abuse is never from Him and is always an indication of the presence of demonic activity. Satan seeks to destroy you and ultimately bring death on any level ... emotionally, financially, relationally and physically ... even mentally.

But our Heavenly Father is love. God is love. He is always love. His love never fails. His love is not measured out. He supplies you with everything you need to prosper and overflow in every way. He loves hanging out with you. He loves doing new adventures with you. He loves to promote you. He loves watching the Holy Spirit teach you how to do life better. You make Him happy. He takes full responsibility for guiding you and protecting you. Whenever the enemy succeeds in convincing you of a lie, your Father jealously puts a plan in place to restore you to truth, all the while healing any wounds in your heart that allowed the lie to enter. He always believes in you and always rises up to defend you.

We are never left orphaned. Jesus promised *He would not leave us as orphans, but that He would come to us*.[8] When He was on the cross, and He willingly allowed the weight of our sin to be placed upon Him, it caused Him to be separated from His Father. It caused Him to become orphaned in our place. While He was in the garden of Gethsemane, He was deeply distressed, troubled, and overwhelmed with sorrow because He knew what faced Him. He was going to endure that separation.[9] He cried out loudly from the cross, *"My God, my God, why have you forsaken me?"*[10] He became orphaned. He became orphaned in our place, so that we can never, never be separated from His love.

ONE WORD FROM the LORD

One word from the Lord changes everything. Earlier I shared words I had written in my journal:

> *I long deeply to go home. I see the Father on a porch sitting in a rocker. I want Him to hold me on His lap, and rock me and rock me and whisper in my ear, "You did good, Patty. You did good."*
>
> *I began to pray that the Lord would come and take me. On the second night, I fell asleep praying that. In the middle of that night, I was awakened from a sound sleep as I felt His Presence in the room. I sat upright in my bed, listening, and in my heart I clearly heard Him speak these words, "This day I have set before you life and death. Now choose life, Patty, so that you and your children may live."*[11]

He sees. He cares. He comes in your need. He draws you to Himself so that you, and your children, and your marriage, and the plans that He has for your life and future may all live and flourish. He is the God of Life ... Resurrection Life. All that emanates from Him is Life. Below is a prophetic word that was given to me about ten years into my journey. It was a profound, profound ray of hope for me that brought His tender affirmation and gloriously enlivened my heart with resurrection life. At the close of receiving this word that long ago day, my spirit erupted with a loud, piercing cry of liberation. For those whose pilgrimage has been likened unto mine, these words belong to you also. He speaks them over your life today. Read them over and over. Receive the Lord's healing deliverance as it washes over you. Turn your face toward the coming brightness, and allow yourself to feel His sunshine reaching for you. You are His. He is saying:

> *Truly I have sent a refreshing your way. Not a refreshing, a resurrection. I have brought you forth. I've brought you forth from the dead, actually. And when you had given up, and when you had given up and said, "I've just had it all. I've had enough," that's when I reached down and pulled you up and said, "Yes, there's life here. There's life here." And daughter, I've brought you into the resurrection life and the resurrection power. That's what I want you to grasp hold of. And I do not want defeat admitted ever again. I don't want you ever to even look and say, you know, that the grave would be more comfortable than where I am. But daughter I*

want you to look up, look up, for the days, the days are looking brighter. The star, the star, the morning star Jesus Christ, is shining brighter. It's getting brighter and your walk will get brighter. You have passed through the valley of the shadow of death, and you have come through that, and I want you to understand you're walking out of that, into the sunlight. Keep pursuing. Yes, O yes! Amen! Yes amen! Hallelujah! Nothing is ahead like what was in the past. No torment like there … there was a severe torment in the past. There's none of that ahead.

the INVITATION

Our choices matter. Our choices have reverberations far beyond ourselves, and our sin affects others, beyond ourselves, in very tangible ways. We do not live life on an island unto ourselves. When Danny chose selfishness, that choice sowed seeds of very real pain into Mandy's little heart. We need to respect this dynamic. And, although it hardly seems fair, we must respect and acknowledge the truth that this dynamic operates even when we are the one who is being wrongly treated, because the way that we choose to respond when wrongly treated has far reaching consequences, for life or for death.

Let us employ this truth to work on our behalf and on the behalf of those we love. If, when treated wrongly, we justify ourselves to respond in ways that do not align with our true identity in God, we will affect others negatively. If we choose disappointment, regret, sadness, grief, self-pity, depression, passivity, bitterness, anger, hate, revenge, pride, fear, unbelief, rejection, inferiority, shame, torment, self-condemnation or guilt, we will give ground to the enemy. Contrarily, the liberating truth is that if we respond out of our place of security as His deeply loved child, we disempower the agents of darkness that seek to destroy our homes and families. Our Father's love has empowered us *to overcome evil with good*.[12]

Just one person partnering with God releases a powerfully redemptive domino effect in a family or marriage or relationship.[13] The Holy Spirit plus one believer is a majority. Today the Lord is inviting you to be that one believer in your situation. He is calling you to rise up and be a first fruits offering for the healing of others. God powerfully used a man named Joseph in this way. His brothers hated him and treated him cruelly. But years afterward, Joseph was used to save their lives because of his heart of forgiveness. Joseph said to them, *"Don't be afraid. ... You intended to*

> **One person partnering with God releases a powerfully redemptive domino effect**

harm me, but God intended it for good to accomplish what is now being done, the saving of many lives."[14]

We choose to believe. We choose to respond rightly. We choose Him. We choose life. Again and again we choose life. We are warriors and champions and that is what warriors and champions do. We live right so that those who come after us can live free.

CONCLUSION

You are known in Heaven. The Father dreamed about you before He even created you. Then He fashioned you according to the dream in His heart. Your identity is secure and irrevocable in Him. You are worthy of the identity He has given you. You belong to Him, and He is fully committed to caring for you in every way. He will protect you, He will walk with you, He will never leave you, and when you wander from Him He will come after you. He has plans for you and His plans are good. When you are shaken in any way, again and again He comes to be your Strength, and He whispers tenderly, "My Beloved, choose life!" He is love and you are the object of that love. The Father's true identity and your true identity are intricately bound up together, with no beginning and no end. All of Heaven is cheering for you. You cannot fail.

PRAYER

Father, You are enlarging my understanding of Your goodness. Thank you for coming in my time of need. I choose today to step into Your goodness. I receive Your healing love as the awareness of Your comfort and protection wraps itself around my heart like a warm blanket. Father, I ask You to uncover every lie that I have believed about You and every lie that I have believed about myself. I take back my identity. I want to walk in your truth. Thank You that You are bringing revelation of truth into my heart. I know, Lord Jesus, that You are changing me, and I feel hope. Have your way in my life. Amen

THOUGHTS *for* REFLECTION *and* DISCUSSION

1. What was stirring in your heart as you processed through this chapter?

2. Can you remember a time when believing in the Father's goodness was a struggle for you?

3. What was going on during that time? Are you able to look back and see it differently now?

4. How has the Holy Spirit altered your understanding of Who your Father is for you?

5. How has the Holy Spirit altered your understanding of the Father's very personal intentionality when He created and wired you?
6. Are you beginning to see a new future forming before you? What does it look like?
7. What are you excited about right now? What is the Holy Spirit awakening in your heart?
8. Where do you need to choose life?

Endnotes

1. Psalm 3:3, NIV.
2. Psalm 66:10-12, NIV.
3. Deuteronomy 30:19, NIV.
4. Psalm 18:4-5,16-17, NIV.
5. John 13:3, NIV.
6. Jeremiah 1:5, NIV.
7. Luke 15:4-6, NIV.
8. John 14:18, NIV.
9. Mark 14:34, NIV.
10. Mark15:34, NIV.
11. Deuteronomy 30:19, NIV.
12. Romans 12:21, NIV.
13. Note: There are times when the persistence of unrelenting onslaughts, especially those which do not respond to prayer, can signify other underlying causes at work. Sometimes we can be dealing with generational sin. Wrong choices were made by those who came before us, and the consequences then play themselves out in our own life. My parents' breaking relationship with me is an example of generational sin.
14. Genesis 50:20, NIV.

> *To love someone means to see him as God intended him*
>
> —Fyodor Dostoyevsky

Part Two

ACTIVATING YOUR UNIQUENESS

*For we are His workmanship, created
in Christ Jesus for good works,
which God prepared beforehand,
that we should walk in them.*
—EPHESIANS 2:10, ESV

Chapter Three

Enlisting for The Plan

PART ONE—TESTIMONY

EXITING *my* PAST

Most everyone in the room had now completed their personality test. I tried to calm the swirl of panic rising inside of me as people began excitedly comparing results with one another. It was a simple test with simple directions. For each of the twenty questions, we were instructed to choose the answer that most consistently described our personality. But I was barely through the first few questions when my eye ran anxiously down the page hoping to find just one that I would know how to answer.

The workshop ended, and our little group headed for the ice-cream parlor. We sat around the table as everyone enjoyed laughing and sharing. I felt shut out. Finally someone asked, "Well, Patty, you're being really quiet. How did your test go?" Suddenly anger erupted inside me like a volcano. "I don't have a personality!" I screamed. "I'm all of the answers, all of the time. I'm just whatever people tell me to be. I don't have a personality!"

I was forty-five years old and I wanted off the treadmill and out of the cage. In my heart, I knew I was running as hard as I could at life, and yet I never seemed to get beyond the confines of some mysterious, ignominious cage that held me prisoner. All around me I felt walls trapping me … pushing against me and pushing against me and pushing against me. My heart ached to scale the walls and live outside the cage.

A frustration and agitation began to form within me. I watched as other women, some even younger than me, were doing things that I knew were the very things that I had been created to do. I could feel the rumbling of dreams deep inside of me as they too groaned to be set free. At first the sound was only a faint ripple that could barely be trusted. But the rumble grew more and more insistent and disruptive, intruding abrasively into my fear, and a stubborn spark of faith pushed its tiny hand out from my pitiful ash heap of defeat and ignited the dreams. As if in response to my faith, far out on the distant horizon there began to come into focus a place that was calling my name.

In October, I drove to Charlotte, North Carolina, to attend a conference. Several of the scheduled conference speakers were authors who had deeply mentored me through their books. There was a hurt inside me so big that I could not separate myself from it, and I went to North Carolina with a hunger and desperation to hear God's voice. The crowd there was large and, as so often happened, I felt lonely and out of place. Familiar emotions swirled inside me as once again I wrestled with the hopelessness that there were no answers for me. On the last day of the conference, I was standing outside with the crowds of people who were returning from lunch. As we stood there waiting for the doors to re-open, my heart was feeling anxious and unsettled.

I went off by myself and found some welcome shade beneath the branches of a large tree. In a show of impatience, I stomped my foot. "Lord Jesus," I said, "this is Patty. From Ohio. Lord, I drove all the way down here because I need to hear a word from You. Lord, my heart has been ripped apart, and I don't know how to go on. Lord, I'm asking you to speak to me. I don't care how hard a word it is or even if you have to discipline me. I just want to hear Your voice."

I went into the auditorium and took an aisle seat halfway down as the musicians were beginning to play. As we entered worship, I could strongly sense the Presence of the Lord behind me. I turned, and in my spirit, I could see the Lord far at the back of the room. I could see Him begin to come forward, striding down the aisle with great purpose and appointment, His gaze fixed straight ahead. He was dressed in a tunic of royalty, majestic and kingly. His demeanor was that of a warrior, *a mighty man come to triumph over his enemies*.[1] When He reached the place where I was standing, He stopped beside me and turned to face me. "I'm moving on, Patty. If you choose to stay here and nurse your wounds, I'll be gone. It's time to get down off my lap." And that quickly, He moved on.

His words jolted me ... arrested me. He was offering me an ultimatum. And He had made the ultimatum very clear. His lap was what I longed for and where I wanted to be. Yet He was asking me to follow Him into an unknown future. He was indeed moving on and it was my choice if I would be with him. Down off His lap ... into my future ... I could not fathom it. Quietly, my heart whispered yes to Him.

As the gathering was drawing to a close, an invitation was given for anyone to come forward who had not previously been personally ministered to. The line was long, the evening was late, and I had a lengthy trip ahead of me in the morning. But none of it mattered. I had come to hear from God. When the conference leader began to pray for me, she said, "The Lord is showing me that your inner man is in great turmoil. You are hungry and starved for the Word of God. The Lord wants to feed you with His Word." I did not understand, and I shared with her that I spent large amounts of time reading His Word. "Oh, yes," she replied, "the Lord shows me that you are receiving great knowledge of His Word in your mind, but it is not reaching your spirit man. It's as if you can't receive good news."

The following evening I pulled the car into our garage and carried my suitcase up the stairs to our bedroom. I was home. Home to the same rooms where I had wept my tears ... home to the same familiar turmoil waiting to swallow me again. But I knew that I stood at a divine juncture. The Lord had seen that young woman standing under the tree. He had seen her stomp her foot and had heard her desperate cry. And He had answered from heaven. Etched in my heart was the picture of Jesus as He had moved away from me and headed on. He wanted me with Him. Of that I was certain. And I was also certain of this: that my spirit man was about to receive a long overdue banquet of good news as I faced into the future and ran hard after Him.

AWAKENING to MY FUTURE

The Lord had not forgotten the dreams that had begun to stir down deep inside of me. He knew that my future was hidden inside those dreams, and He was about to turn the rumble into a seismic roar. A few years later, again in the fall, I drove to Nashville, Tennessee, for a conference called Women on the Frontline. I longed passionately to be on the frontline for God's Kingdom. Even so, I did not realize the significance of this conference for my life. God was about to infuse me with a jolt of spiritual voltage that would make shambles of my old paradigms.

I do not remember exactly when it happened, but at some point early on an older woman took the platform. She was introduced as Eileen Vincent. She was at once captivating and delightfully mischievous, and it was instantly apparent that the Holy Spirit adored her. She said that she had read about this conference at her home in Texas and that God had told her she was to come and speak. How outrageously and refreshingly audacious! And that was exactly why the Lord had brought her.

Eileen shared her amazing testimony of how God unexpectedly lifted her out of the place that others had defined for her and thrust her into His dreams for her life. She shared how she and her husband had traveled for years, into many nations, doing ministry in a time when it was considered improper for women to preach. The chairs on the platform were all reserved for men. "Women could share," she said, her eyes twinkling, "but not preach. And that, only if they had a hat on!"

With her fiery and passionate style, Eileen not only brought her message, but she was her message. I drank that night not only from her words but from the bold impact of her life. With great conviction, she shared the following testimony that God had given her to tell. I relate it here in my own words with her permission.

One evening, as she and her husband were driving to a revival meeting, Eileen could sense that her husband was not feeling any particular thought or direction concerning God's heart for the service. "You don't have the word, do you?" she inquired in her British accent.

"No," he replied.

There was a long silence.

"You have it, don't you?" he said.

"Yes," she lamented, just having returned from South Korea and still feeling the overflow of all that God had done there. "But what difference does it make? For I am not allowed to preach." But that night it made all the difference. When they arrived at the gathering, Alan had a chair placed on the platform for Eileen. And when it came time that night for the word to be released, he introduced Eileen in his place.

"I had my hat on," Eileen confessed, "but I didn't share. Honey, I preached!"

In the days that followed, she was nearly overcome with condemnation for what she had done and convinced that she had disgraced her Lord and Savior. For days she wept, after which Jesus, the Lover of her soul, came and spoke to her. "Eileen," He said, "the gifts that I have given to you do not belong to you. And Eileen, the gifts that I have given to you do not belong to the men. Eileen, the gifts that I have given to you belong to Me."

Tears welled in my eyes that night as the Holy Spirit hovered over the weary waters of my heart. The leather straps of man-made doctrines were coming unloosed. Wholeness and restoration were seeping into the fragmented shards of my personality as the Great Physician moved skillfully to redeem all that the years had stolen. Warm, healing rays of hope hung their pegs firmly in my heart. Eileen's testimony had unmercifully shattered the walls of my prison, and fireworks exploded inside of me as the dreams that I had felt guilty for believing in now stood confidently erect and at attention. An unshakable sense of purpose and destiny began to take hold of me.

the DEAL is SEALED

There are four books in my personal library that have carried me in season and out of season. They are the biographies and sermons of Aimee Semple McPherson, Kathryn Johanna

Kuhlman, Smith Wigglesworth, and Maria Woodworth-Etter. The picture on the cover of each book is the same. The servant of God stands, one hand holding the opened Scriptures, the other hand upraised to heaven as the Word is boldly preached. Although the pages of each book are marked and worn, and have been read many times, it has always been the covers that have arrested my heart. Time after time, when I would feel I could not go on, I would go to the shelf, pull down the books, hold them tightly to my heart and weep.

I had not understood in those times that deep was calling unto deep. I had not known that the same eternal streams of glory that flowed through those pictures were gurgling in my own heart. On the Sunday morning following the conference in Nashville, I sat down in our usual spot at church and opened the bulletin. My eyes fastened upon the words, Preaching with Power, and my heart did a somersault! The class was being offered through a local Bible college. I filled out the enrollment form and wrote my check.

As I took a seat on the first night of class, I watched as the room filled up with young men. The weeks passed as I attended the classes, read the required textbooks and completed the required assignments. On the final night of class, we were each given the opportunity to preach for five minutes. One of the young men asked if our grade would be affected if we exceeded the time. I had not thought about that. And I did not care. The yearning, the fervor, the ache to preach burned inside me, as if it had been shut up within me for a lifetime.

I was last. As I came to the podium, I was flooded with a deep sense of joy and strong personal identity. I knew, as I stood there, that God had called me to deliver His Word into the earth. I had cherished and fed upon His Word for over twenty years, and I preached from the very wells of salvation that lived within me. I could feel the Lord's tangible pleasure with me all the way as if He too had been waiting for this night. When I finished, one of the instructors stretched out his arm, pointed his finger at me, and declared, "Woman, God's called you to preach. And you can preach in my pulpit anytime you want."

> **I could feel the Lord's tangible pleasure with me as if He too had been waiting for this night**

In the months and years to come, God solidified my assurance of the call. It came in many ways. Mostly it came quietly in my times alone with Him. He tested my heart. He tested my strength. He tested my desire. He weaned me from the fear of man and made note of my quickness to obey His Voice. Knowing full well what He was asking, I remember the day and the place in our home when I presented myself before Him and invited Him to clothe me in the call.

PART TWO—INSIGHTS

TRUST RESTORED
a Place *on* His Lap

There is a word that is used by the Lord in the Hebrew Scriptures that has become absolutely beautiful to me. Just the word itself, over the years, has again and again been a fountain of healing for me. The word is bos, and it means to be ashamed, confounded or disappointed, to be disgraced, to be kept waiting or to be deceived. It often occurs in scriptural contexts of humiliation, public disgrace, and shattered human emotions. Bos denotes confusion, embarrassment or dismay when things do not turn out as expected. Sometimes there is a strong connotation of guilt or disillusionment and a broken spirit.

I cannot count the times that I have read these words. I would especially linger over the phrases *shattered human emotions* and *dismay when things do not turn out as expected*, because that was the place where it seemed that the sword had most painfully pierced my own heart. Knowing that my Father had a word for all of it brought me such comfort and assured me that He truly understood.

Some of you have been through your own seasons of trauma where you have experienced indescribable wounding, broken trust and broken relationships. There has been mental anguish, emotional anguish, confusion, the delayed fulfillment of dreams, sowing that has produced no reaping, grief, loss, regret, betrayal and devastation. Some of you have even sensed that God has abandoned you. What are the phrases that arrested your heart as you considered the word *bos*?

My own heart and soul have experienced profound dismay as I have journeyed through my story. I have been dismayed by the intensity of the ordeal. I have been dismayed by the duration of the ordeal. I have been dismayed by the unyielding persistence of the ordeal in the face of prolonged and persistent prayer. I felt that I was living off the grid. And I believe that many of you have felt these same things.

It is important that we truthfully acknowledge our pain. If we are passing through the valley of the shadow of death, it should never be painted over or denied as less than what it is. That is spiritual bravado and a very hollow form of make-believe. Your Father did not do these things to you. It is the thief that comes to destroy,[2] and Jesus comes to destroy the thief's work.[3] You need to know and be able to clearly name exactly what it is that the enemy has stolen from you. If you don't know, get a piece of paper and take inventory. Write it down. Has the enemy stolen your marriage? Has he stolen your children? Has he stolen your health or your finances? Has he stolen your laughter? Does it seem that he has stolen your future? Write it all down. It will actually energize you, bring clarity, and give direction to your conversations with the Lord. You need to be unashamedly honest and acknowledge your pain to Jesus. That is what I was doing when I stomped my foot under that tree.

It is also critical that at some juncture we learn to receive the Lord's comfort. Without it, we cannot move on. We have to know that we know that He is with us and has been with us, and that we are safe because He is there. Being comforted means that we must find our place on His lap. We must come there often. We must know, in a very personal way, the strength and security of His arms around us. We must lean in close, hungrily pressing our face into the earthiness of His simple Shepherd's garment. It is our right to be there. We are His. Our healing commences there. Acquiescing to be held is a gesture of humility, and humility is always rewarded in the Kingdom.

Remembering that the Father has purposed for you to fly, you will begin to understand that His lap is a strategic high place. His lap is actually one of the best places from which to take flight. Throughout our healing, whenever we humble ourselves and crawl up onto His lap, taking flight becomes inevitable. So we come as often as we want. But we do not stay there, because the aerodynamics of flight render it impossible. Our healing begins there, but there is more.

Receiving *good* News

God is always after our heart. He is always more interested in changing our hearts than in vindicating our circumstances. Once His surgery is complete, our hearts will have aligned with His heart, and then the other will follow. For endless years, the only thing that the Lord seemed intent on changing was me. I spent a lot of time on His lap as He did His work in me. But that night in Charlotte, at the conference, He abruptly served notice on that season of my life. He has plans for us. He is moving on, and we must move on with Him. We cannot stay there in our pain and nurse our wounds. Our tears must end, and we must be weaned from our perpetual neediness.

> **Our tears must end, and we must be weaned from our perpetual neediness**

This is a day when God is moving quickly. He is here to restore you, and it is going to happen quickly. If you do not already know that you are called, then know it now. Your holding this book is evidence that the Father has called you. He knows you picked up this book, and He is going to meet you. At the conference that afternoon, He came right to the place where I was standing. He came and stopped right there at the aisle where I stood engulfed in my pain. He let me know that my longtime lease for parking space on His lap had expired, and He issued His invitation to follow Him. He knew I was coming to that conference, and he met me there. He knows you picked up this book, and he will meet you in the same way. He knows where He is taking you. He knows how it is going to look. He is excited about it.

Go sit on His lap and dump it all out. Don't ask why you had to go through it. Don't say it wasn't fair. Just rest there in Him. Stay there until you want to go, then return again. The Lord is going to wash your wounds. You are going to be changed and made whole. It is there in the arms of His love that He is going to restore your trust again. He is bringing you forth into a place in Him, where once again you will be able to hold forth your heart to others expecting nothing in return. You are going to find yourself saying yes to Him, and when we say yes to Him, our future is born. He is going to set His hand to your life and bring you through, and bring you forward, into a destiny and a purpose. You will hope in Him and you will not be disappointed (*bos*).[4]

Our hearts can endure anything as long as we can assign purpose to it. Know that God will never waste anything that you have gone through, and all of the enemy's work will ultimately serve God's intentions for you. It is a great honor that He has trusted you with pain. It shows a lot about what God sees in you and what He wants to bring out of you for others. Your pain is your passport. It is going to take you places you would have never dreamed you would go, and it will open doors for you that otherwise would have remained locked.

Receiving good news is an instantaneous transaction between your heart and the Lord's. You are saying, "I am with you Lord. I believe." When it is not going well, when it is hard, that is where we learn to trust Him, and where He learns to trust us. We are able to trust that He sees more, and that He knows more. We are saying to Him that to become like Him through our present circumstances is a higher priority than just receiving a successful result. Receive the good news. Trust and expect good things to happen.

Again, I am sharing below a prophetic word that was given to me along the way. I know these words belong to you also, and the Lord speaks them over your life today. Grab His outstretched hand and prepare for take-off.

> For the Lord would say, *"Daughter, even know that I'm even causing trust to be restored within your heart says the Lord. You would have even walked through some situations even in past years where there would have been broken trust with people, and it would have even brought a great wounding to your heart. But know this day that I'm even causing your trust in me to be re-instilled in different ways. Know that as you hope in me surely you will not be disappointed.*

"I'm beginning to even stir vision within your heart afresh and anew. There would have even been that season of time that you would have walked through, and it would have even seemed like every dream and every vision would have been crushed for a season, but know that I'm even setting my hand to your life in this season of time.

"I'm bringing you through and I'm bringing you forward even into a destiny and a purpose. Know that there's even been some challenges of fear that have warred against you, but I'm even coming to break the power of fear. Even in some night seasons the enemy would have come to torment you even in some areas about the days ahead and what to expect. But I'm destroying even the power of the torment, and I'm even releasing you to expect good things to happen. Know that even as I begin to open some new doors of relationship to you you're gonna begin to step through those doors, and you're gonna find that there's gonna be trust established once again within your heart not only with me but with people on a new level," says God.

God is UNFAILINGLY *redemptive.*

—LARRY RANDOLPH

UNDER CONSTRUCTION
Interior Renovation

So, this book is about you. It is about you getting into the driver's seat and living out His storyline for your life. It is about you tapping into the plans that He buried inside your spirit. It is not about all the other people in your life, or better yet, in your car. Yes, they are there with you. But you are the one that has enrolled in His Royal Flight Academy. The Lord takes your yes very seriously. If you truly embark on this great adventure, your victory is assured. Jesus' invitation is for whosoever, and He turns no one away. He sees where He is taking you, He knows His plan for getting you there, and with great love and kindness, He will prepare you to be able to stand victoriously once you get there.

Your *yes* releases and activates a brand new dynamic between you and the Lord, and subsequently, He is going to now begin interacting with you differently. It had only been a short season of time since I had said yes to the Lord, when He strategically brought Eileen to the conference that I was attending in Nashville. Eileen shared how God lifted her out of the old place and cannon-shot her into the new. God knew that her testimony had the power to bust my old paradigms wide open. He planned the whole thing, and before that night was over, I was in the new place.

God is going to orchestrate circumstances for you that will be like visual aids. He is going to set divine encounters in motion for the purpose of dismantling faulty mindsets that you have been operating out of. The Holy Spirit wants to bring fresh truth to you. He is going to be teaching you a new way of seeing, a new way of thinking, and even a new way of speaking. The Holy Spirit is about to become your most enthusiastic Friend and Helper.

We must not come to God just in a functional sense, just to be rescued or for Him to solve a problem. Our situation is really not about the problem. Rather, the problem is about Him and me. It is about our walking together. He wants relationship with us, and He wants to do life together with us. God's first priority is going to be getting inside your heart so that He can rearrange all the furniture. He wants to redesign the landscape of your heart. He wants to haul away all the debris from your past and paint the walls with joy.

Jesus never looks back to where you came from. In Him, everything is new. In Him, all possibilities are permissible to you. You are not a fixer-upper. You are a brand new house.

Trust in His guidance and do not be of two minds. If you make a wrong turn, he will adjust your course. He knows you are going to stumble and make mistakes, but He is not worried about it. He believes in you, and on your most stupid days His kindness empowers you to simply dust yourself off and have another go at it. You are stepping into a process and a relationship with Him, a place of freedom and security where you will begin to enjoy and celebrate who you are. You will be in the driver's seat.

Erecting New Walls

The transformation of a life from brokenness to wholeness is quite a profound occurrence, and it requires great resolution and courage. All the powers of hell stand ready to defeat us at every turn. We will fight one battle to get free, and we will fight another battle to stay free. The apostle Paul spoke plainly: *Finally, let no one cause me trouble, for I bear on my body the marks of Jesus.*[5] Each one of us will bear internal scars testifying of our own personal warfare to *take off our old self and put on the new self.*[6] Over and over, we must put this new thing on. We keep putting it on until it stays on. Each time we put it on, we become more acclimated to it, and we can move in it with less effort. Put on what you are learning right now. Keep putting it on. Keep putting it on until it stays on. Practice, practice, practice.

We are in a war. We have a very real opponent. He will seek to make us weary. He will seek to demoralize us. With time, you may question if the journey is worth it. In order to repel the enemy's lies, you will have to erect new walls around your heart. One of the walls that will protect your heart is hunger. Only love will bring you home in this conflict of wills; nevertheless, hunger will serve you well. *To the hungry even what is bitter tastes sweet.*[7] You must want the victory. You must hunger for it. The possibility of never taking flight must be uncompromisingly distasteful to you, and you must settle in your heart that even what is bitter will only serve to reward you.

The second wall that will guard you heart is faith. You must be able to see where the Father wants to take you and have faith that He indeed can and will take you there. Faith is the currency of the Kingdom and gives you the power to see the invisible and move toward it. Whenever a mountain presents itself before you and seeks to resist you, faith will go around the mountain, spring up it, or run straight through it. At times, faith will simply *speak to the mountain to go throw itself into the sea.*[8] Faith is your shield and will extinguish all the flaming arrows of the evil one.[9] Lean in to Jesus and position yourself to hear His voice. Find key words in Scripture and begin to build your life around them. Expect the Lord to give you personal scriptures and prophetic words to live by. You will need them to fortify your walls. Ask Him for these things and He will graciously supply them.

Below is a random sampling of different things that I have journaled over the years while going through the remolding of my own heart. Allow these to speak to you: saying no to double-mindedness, learning to rejoice in all circumstances, cultivating an expectation of continual upgrade, being slow to speak, walking in love, basking in his majesty, celebrating his grace, enjoying the learning, knowing when to speak and when to refrain from speaking, knowing when to put my heart out there and when to let it rest with God, not thinking I am too old and that destiny has passed me by, knowing I must respond to the Holy Spirit rather than to people, allowing my life to be given away, putting into practice that wisdom is better than logic, becoming extravagantly generous, becoming warmly kind and merciful, being a good listener, practicing my peace, becoming someone who creates empowerment and growth for others, being outrageously free to laugh too much, developing a new vocabulary and developing a heavenly mindset that governs my own life, my choices, and the way I see.

the INVITATION

Every living being is created with great care and attention by the Master Designer. *He has a plan for us to prosper and to have hope and a future.*[10] Our hearts know that. And whenever we lose our way and default to the wrong storyline for our life, our hearts know that too.

> *"Your spirit has a memory of your future inside of it that your mind is trying to catch up to. You were pre-known by God, and He wrote down all your days before you ever got here. He said, 'I*

know the plans I have for you ...' One function of the gift of prophecy is to tap into those plans buried inside the human spirit and reveal them to the hearer. I call this hitting the 'sweet spot,' because even though the person didn't know the plans in their mind, their spirit will recognize it, causing an outburst of praise to Almighty God."

—JENNIFER EIVAZ

The Lord is inviting you into relationship. He is standing in your future beckoning you to allow the eyes of your heart to see your inheritance in Him. He is the Author of the dreams that live inside you, and He is calling you to trust in His love and to say yes to the process of stepping into the right story line. He longs to walk together with you allowing your heart and His heart to become one.

God wants your heart and His heart to become one

In his book *Tell Your Heart to Beat Again,* Dutch Sheets shares the following story. "During an open-heart surgery that my brother, Tim, was allowed to witness, the patient's heart had been stopped from beating. However when it came time to restart it, despite repeated attempts, the medical staff was unable to get the heart to beat again. Finally, although the patient was obviously unconscious, the surgeon leaned over and said into the patient's ear, 'We need your help. We cannot get your heart going. Tell your heart to start beating.' Immediately, as incredible as it sounds, the patient's heart began to beat again."

God believes in you. He put His dream within you, and He is leaning over you and saying into your ear, "We need your help up here. A lot has happened to you, and your heart has stopped beating like it used to. You have gotten separated from the dream. We need you to believe again. Tell your heart to beat again." The Lord will be faithful to you, and He will watch over what He has birthed in you. He will protect it and bring it to completion.[11] He knows who He made you to be and He will empower you to become it. *Slowly, steadily, surely, the time approaches when the vision will be fulfilled. If it seems slow, do not despair, for these things will surely come to pass. Just be patient! They will not be overdue a single day!*[12]

CONCLUSION

You are right now positioned before a doorway of change. On this side of the door is your past; on the other side is your future. On this side of the door is defeat; on the other side is your unique storyline. On this side of the door is the passenger's seat; on the other side is the driver's seat. On this side of the door is sitting on His lap; on the other side is taking flight. On this side of the door are tears; on the other side is laughter. On this side of the door is a perpetual victim mindset; on the other side is doing life with Him. This side is your no; the other side is your yes. The Lord is moving on, and your response is needed. He wants you with Him, and He is listening for your yes. Receive the good news, choose life and trust again.

PRAYER

Lord Jesus, thank You for the place where I stand today. Thank You for opening my eyes to be able to see beyond where I am and for giving me faith to believe that with You I can go forward. The journey has been hard, Lord, and long. I have felt torn and ripped apart. It means everything to me that You have been there through it all, Lord, and that you are healing my wounds and will cause all of it to work together for good. I give you all the disappointment and regret. I surrender it to You, I say yes, and I choose to walk with you and dream again. I am excited about our new relationship. I trust that You are bringing me through and bringing me forward into a destiny and a purpose. Have Your way in my heart. Change me, Holy Spirit. Amen.

THOUGHTS *for* REFLECTION *and* DISCUSSION

1. Do you find it difficult to receive good news? What do you believe has caused this?

2. What are some of the dreams that rumble around on the inside of you? What would you like God to do with those dreams? Can you tell Him that right now?

3. Have you suffered broken trust with people? Have you suffered broken trust with God? How did this chapter bring healing and hope to you?

4. Share an example of what putting your new self on would look like for you?

5. On a scale of 1 to 10, with 10 being the most intense, what would you say is the level of your hunger to do life with the Lord?

Endnotes

1. Isaiah 42:13, NIV.
2. John 10:10, NIV.
3. 1 John 3:8, NIV.
4. Isaiah 49:23, NIV.
5. Galatians 6:17, NIV.
6. Colossians 3:9-10, NIV.

7. Proverbs 27:7b, NIV.
8. Mark 11:23, NIV.
9. Ephesians 6:16, NIV.
10. Jeremiah 29:11, NIV.
11. Philippians 1:6, NIV.
12. Habakkuk 2:3, TLB.

> We can never know who or what we are till we know at least something of what God is.
>
> —A.W. Tozer

Chapter Four

Letting Your Heart Come Forward

PART ONE—TESTIMONY

the BREWING STORM

The wedding gown hung quite gracefully on the mannequin, peering out from the display window as we parked our car on downtown Eleventh Avenue. I waited while my mother clinked her change into the curbside parking meter then followed her through the double doors that led into Meyer Jonasson's. In my years of growing-up, my visits to this distinguished clothing store had been only a few. I felt awkward.

The gown from the display window was brought to the dressing room for me to try on. The front was deeply yellowed from long exposure to the harsh rays of sunlight, and the dress was drastically marked down to ten dollars. The gown fit, my mother paid the money, it was placed into a beautiful box and we took it home.

We went into the house and I carried the box to my bedroom. Suddenly my mother was behind me. Reaching out her hand and roughly taking hold of my wrist, she twisted it sharply. Her teeth were clenched and she snarled, "So help me, if you're pregnant, I'll make you walk down that aisle in black." The gown, the beautiful gown was heavy in my hands.

The enemy preys upon our vulnerability as little children. In a time when our hearts are young and unprotected, he violates our innocence and stealthily erects his iron castles within our souls, leaving us rent asunder from the loving-kindness of heaven from whence we came and longing to find our way back.

My life seemed almost always overshadowed by fear. Fear is the dominant emotion in all of my memories. I understood that I was to concentrate intently at all times upon doing the right thing, because there was always the looming fear that I could do the wrong thing. Life was serious. There were fearful nights of shouting and anger when my brother would come to my room, and together we would huddle in the dark under my bedspread, comforted and made brave by one another's love. I knew that the next day and every day after, I must be careful, very careful, to obey all the rules. I worked hard to do everything right. At the same time an escalating anger simmered within me along with an insatiable hunger for love.

My mother did not encourage conversation. My only assignment was obedience. My brother died while we were teenagers, and I became an only child. I married his closest friend. "Are you sure you want to marry her?" my mother asked him. "Why, she is the most selfish person on earth. Surely you don't think you can live with her!"

> "Are you sure you want to marry her? She is the most selfish person on earth ..."

When I gave my life to the Lord, I came to Him just as I was—full of determination to do everything right. But as I walked with Him and as our relationship grew deeper, I repeatedly found myself up against a rock wall. He was not like others. Loving others was the only thing He required, and I did not know how to love. Yet I wanted more than anything to please Him.

I did not, indeed could not, perceive the length of the journey that stood facing me. The sincerity of my heart could not be questioned, and yet I could not deliver the goods. Progress was slow, and condemnation haunted me as I confronted the gaping hole of inadequacy in my own heart. I battled against raging insecurity and a fearful sense of isolation as I began to feel hopelessly different, ashamed, and defeated. More and more I was convinced that something was wrong with me and that it could never be fixed.

Throughout this time, the Lord was building something very solid within me. Over and over He saw my heart and invested in it. And each time I responded, He invested some more. Unseen and in secret, the Lord was one by one dislodging the stones that had calcified my heart. Even so, decades would pass before the root of bitterness that had poisoned me would be completely pulled out.

the ERUPTION

The estrangement between my mother and me grew worse as my own children grew older. We lived hours apart, and things were strained whenever we were together. I always felt her disapproval. My parents were angry about my relationship with the Lord and angry with my failure as a mother. During our visits, I was belittled, cursed, slapped and at times ordered to leave their home. If I tried to speak, my mother would hold her hands over her ears and scream at me, "Don't you ever speak to me like that in my house!"

During the long dark years that settled over our own family and household, my parents refused to visit us. Their letters of condemnation came regularly in the mailbox, and my hands would shake and my stomach would recoil in knots as I carried the letters into the house. I knew that if I did not read them I would incur their punishment.

The Bible says that *we know in part*.[1] I really believe that we also remember only in part. My mother walked through all of these things that I am writing about from her own side of the story ... a side that only she can remember and a side that will never be written. You are reading my side, and she has given me her blessing to tell it. The story of my mother and me is a love story of two very crippled women who were tenderly and passionately pursued by the stubborn mercy of a Savior longing to make them both whole. My mother and father lived inside their own prison of pain and that prison was built in part by me.

My mother had been widowed only a few weeks before Christmas arrived. So my husband and I traveled home to get her and bring her back to spend the holidays with us. We had all bought little gifts for her, and they were waiting for her under our tree. Benjamin, our young grandson, joined us on the long trip, and we arrived at my mother's cottage in the early evening.

Benjamin and his grandpa staked out their territory in the spare bedroom and happily began to settle into their pajamas. I stayed in the kitchen with my mother while she puttered. Soon Benjamin, having eaten a very early dinner, wandered out from the bedroom hungry for a snack, and his great-grandmother offered him an orange. Climbing up on the stool, he ate his orange, and then ran off to rejoin Grandpa. But my mother was upset that Benjamin had been wasteful with the orange. She ordered me to call him back to the kitchen and make him eat it properly, which for her included all of the rind.

My stomach began to churn as I stood silently. I felt trapped. It was always this way. I was for peace, but she was for war. "You're not going to do it, are you?" she suddenly screamed at me. "You're so high and mighty that you don't have to listen to anyone!"

"Mom, it's alright," I said softly and respectfully. "He hasn't ever been required to eat it that way. In his mind it wasn't anything wrong." I smiled as I cleaned off the counter and I said, "It's just a generational thing."

I went into the bathroom and began to get myself ready for bed. But my mother came in behind me, pushed her face into mine, and began screaming again. Again I felt trapped and again I answered her softly, but she began to grab me. All of a sudden rage rose up within me ... hot, ugly rage. I took hold of my mother's neck with both my hands and literally felt dizzy from the dark hatred that began to swirl around me. I stood staring into her face … the face that somehow, even after all these years of tears and earnest prayer, I could not get free from. Then slowly my hands loosened their grip, and I let go.

By now Hollis and Benjamin were aware. My mother was eighty years old and very frail. She dropped herself to the floor in the hallway and began gasping for Hollis to help her, screaming frantically that her own daughter was trying to kill her. Hollis did what he could to calm everything, but the air was filled with tension. My mother grew extremely cold and stony, and ordered us to leave.

The night was late as we carried our suitcases out of the cottage and loaded them back into the car. I tried to go inside again to hold her, to attempt some sense of reconciliation, but her porch door was locked and she would not respond to my knocking. I got into our car, and Hollis slowly backed out, turning west onto the lonely, winding mountain road.

When we came to an old, dirt pull-off, I asked him to stop. I reached for Benjamin and held him tight in my arms. I asked if we could go back. Surely we needed to go back. She was all alone, and I was frightened for her. But we knew it would only make things worse. Something very final had occurred. Her door was closed … perhaps forever.

the ESTRANGEMENT

For weeks my dreams tormented me. Night after night I woke up wrestling, my arms wildly flailing the air. We were severed from one another, and I was numb with the weight of it. The days dragged by as if all of life had ceased. The sickness of my own heart was like an incurable wound, and despair flirted with me as I stood face to face with the truth that anything so dark and evil could live inside me.

Yet all the time the Lord's arms were holding me tightly. I understood that He had seen this day from afar and now rejoiced to welcome its coming ... that He had been preparing me for a long time. At last, one morning I awoke and knew what I had to do. I showered, packed a bag, and gathered together my mother's unopened Christmas gifts. I stood in our kitchen while Hollis prayed with me, shared his words of wisdom, and blessed me to go. Then I climbed into our van and headed to my mom's.

For hours I traveled in silence. Then, turning onto the road that led up over the mountain, I knew it was time. I was remembering a story that Corrie ten Boom shares in her autobiography, *The Hiding Place*. Corrie's family had provided refuge for the Jews in Holland during the Holocaust. When Corrie was a little girl, her father had promised her that God would always provide her ticket whenever she needed to board the train. When she needed it, it would be there. It was time, and I needed my ticket.

"Lord Jesus," I prayed, "I'm asking You to give me a love for my mother. Lord Jesus, I don't have any of my own, and I'm asking You to give it to me. I'm about to board the train, Lord. In just a short time, I'll be standing on her porch and I need my ticket. I'm asking You, Lord Jesus, to put Your love for my mother into my heart."

All of a sudden, right there in the van, the words of John shot up from deep within me. *My command is this: Love each other as I have loved you.*[2] As I have loved you … as I have loved you … as I have loved you. The words rolled over and over in my mind like a powerful cascading waterfall. They were charged with electricity as my spirit man rose up to lay hold of the revelation. The Lord was not asking me to love my mother the way that He loved her. He was asking me to love her **as He had loved me**.

It was profound. Absolutely profound! Yes, yes! Oh, yes, yes! That was a love I knew. Oh, how I knew that love! That was the love that had brought me up out of darkness. That was the love that had carried me when I could not put one foot in front of another. When I had cried out for the grave, when the well within me had run bone dry, when the hurt and the pain had caused me to lash out against an unseen enemy, that was the love that had put a song in my heart and taught my feet to dance. That was the love, oh, that was the love that had made me whole again. Tears streamed down my face, and my heart began to overflow with brokenness. I knew I could give that love to my mother.

That was the love that had the power to heal both of us.

the RESTORATION

I pulled into town and found a small market where I could refresh myself. Snow was falling, and it was bitter cold as I turned down my mother's lane, parked the van, and made my way up her front walkway. The grey afternoon snow was quickly growing even heavier as I knocked on her door.

When she opened the door and saw me, she turned almost ghostlike as every bit of color drained from her face. Shrieking in terror, she slammed the door shut. The winter wind whipped hard over the porch as I lifted my hand and knocked on the door again. There was no response. I continued to knock and knock, yet still there was no response. Peering through the narrow window, I could see her sitting in her kitchen, the light turned on above her, hunched over her old black sewing machine.

I began to call out to her. "Mom, open the door. Open the door." I kept knocking and calling, and calling and knocking. After a very long, long time, she came to the door.

She screamed at me, enraged, through the window. "Go away! Go away! I don't know you. I have no daughter. I have no daughter anymore. Go away!" And she went back to her sewing.

I kept knocking and calling. "Mom, open the door and let me in. Open the door."

Again she came and began screaming, "What do you want? Why did you come? I don't ever want to see you again."

I said, "Mom, it can't be that way. We have to make things right. We belong to each other."

Angrily she opened the door just enough for me to step inside. "Well, I suppose you can stand inside here," she said in an icy tone, refusing to look at me. "I know its cold out there and you've come a long way." I stepped just inches inside the door and she backed up, standing several feet away from me.

Love overwhelmed my heart and tenderness settled over me. I stood quietly. My mother began to lash out at me with strong verbal accusations as all the anguish inside her had found its target. She carried a lifetime of deep wounds, and many of them had come from me. Where the circle began or ended was of no concern. Finally there was quiet and I spoke. Smiling, and joking lightly, I lovingly teased her, "So there's not anything good about me, Mom?"

"Oh no!" she spewed viciously. "There's nothing good in you! Nothing! Why even your father knew that!"

Again it was quiet. "Mom," I asked, "would it be alright if I held you?" And stepping toward her, I gathered her in my arms. All of my body began to quiver. "I'm so sorry, Mom. I'm so sorry for all the ways that I've hurt you … all the ways that I've disappointed you as a daughter. I'm sorry that Bobby died and that you had to go through that. I'm sorry that Dad died. I'm sorry for all the pain, Mom. I love you." And I held her and could not stop shaking.

My mother was so little. Showing no emotion at all, she stepped back from me, still unable to look at me, and said, "Well … well … why don't you go out and get your suitcase and bring it in. You've traveled a long way. Maybe we can start over again."

I stayed for two days. I never completely stopped shaking, and I never stopped quietly crying. She cooked and we ate. She talked and I listened. The atmosphere seemed almost holy, and I believe there were angels abiding with us. My mom was not able to ever show any emotion and even struggled to accept her Christmas gifts. But she never once made fun of me or showed any disrespect. Surely something new had been born.

Amazingly, the work was not yet complete. Seven years later, there came one last, forceful eruption through which the Lord reached down from heaven, gripped His mighty hand around the entire massive root of unforgiveness in my heart and began violently twisting and pulling on it. He was determined in His heart to unloose its hold on me once and for all, and at last, full and complete forgiveness toward my mother was released.

the BLESSING

There is a death that begins to work in any son or daughter who rejects a parent. Parents have a preserving effect upon their offspring. When a child fails to honor a parent, he cuts himself off from the divine transference of life that flows down through the generations. In a very real sense the child, irrespective of age and aware of it or not, is adrift at sea. All the while the Father watches while His love contends for the turning of our hearts. He has promised that He will restore our broken families. He has promised to *turn the hearts of the fathers to their children, and the hearts of the children to their fathers.*[3]

My mother moved rapidly into Alzheimer's. But during those few months, as she made her short journey into this final stage of her life, Heaven smiled on us and restored all that had been stolen. It seemed the more her mind receded, the more her heart took flight. We fell in love, saying hello to each other for the very first time. And as she slowly faded further and further away, we said goodbye. I found myself weeping over her life in the night. I had asked the Lord to make everything right for her on this side of eternity before calling her to Himself, and in His marvelous faithfulness He supplied our every need.

Somewhere in all of this, while my mom was still able to scuffle about in her walker, there took place a moment that will stand forever isolated on the time line of my life and of my destiny in God. To my mother and to others, the incident bore no particular significance much less eternal weight. But the heart knows its own thirst. And what took place and the words that my mother spoke came from Heaven.

Over a very, long season of time that lasted years and years, God had been restoring my battered soul bit by bit. Eventually there had come a time when I began to enjoy a newfound confidence in who I was. I grew to perceive myself differently and to carry myself differently, and with childlike abandonment, I became aware of a strong stirring of creativity and design that was dancing inside of me. This was new territory for me, and one of the places where it began to show up was in my personal clothing style.

And so there we were that memorable day ... sitting together in her cottage ... when my mom began looking at me. Her eyes were fastened upon my clothing. Suddenly, struggling to pull herself up, she began to hobble toward me. So frail and tiny, inch by inch she pushed her walker all the way across the room, until she was as close as she could come to me. Unsteady, and barely able to stand, she reached out her small, gnarled hand and took hold of my clothing.

She had spent years at her sewing machine, and her hands had worked with so many kinds of materials. Bending her face down, she squinted intensely while she turned the tweedy fabric of my clothing over and over, back and forth, between her fingers. "Oh darling," she said, "your clothes are so … so …" and she labored for the right word … "so different," she gasped, out of breath. Thoroughly spent, she began to stumble backward, and I reached out to catch her.

My heart seemed to freeze in time, as I instantly recognized what had taken place. Quite unconventional to be sure, but oh, I knew what it was! The Lord was granting the parental blessing over my life. *Esau … burst out with a loud and bitter cry and said to his father, "Bless me – me too, my father!"*[4] My mother was speaking the parental blessing that had been held back for years.

Perhaps for some it simply appears all too irregular. But not so. You must learn to eat from the table that is set before you. God was bestowing beauty out of ashes. Love had triumphed. Standing as the link between me and all the generations of my bloodline that had gone before, my mother was now releasing the transference of life and grafting me into the covenantal flow of family blessing.

My mother who had birthed me … my mother who had given me life … my mother who had been chosen for me from before the foundations of the world … It was her voice, her words, declaring over my thirsty heart: "I see your gift. I see this outward expression of that which dances on the inside of you. I was drawn to it, attracted to it, and I have even come up closer that I might see it better. I have touched it and examined it. And I have this to say concerning it: it is different. That which lives inside of you is different. That which God has clothed you in is different. It is different from me. It is different from what I have seen on others. It is so, so different."

My mom had blessed me to be different. She had blessed me to be different! She took the very thing that I had been afraid to embrace and lifted it up to a place of honor. The parental blessing comes with great authority, and time and time again, in the years to come, my mother's words were destined to silence the voice of the enemy over my life.

> **She took the very thing I had been afraid to embrace and lifted it up to a place of honor**

PART TWO – INSIGHTS

KEEPING *no* RECORD *of* WRONGS
His Example

Our journeys through life can become quite messy. But God knows that, and so He is never caught off guard by our broken relationships. He knows that we rarely planned for it to go that way. In fact, Scripture tells us that even when we have been stubborn and turned from Him, He takes us in His arms, bends down to heal us and feed us, and lifts the heavy yokes from our neck.[5] If you have picked up this book and read this far, most likely your relationships with the people in your life fall short of what you are longing for them to be.

God does not want you to remain in that wilderness place. He knows that when we become isolated from each other, going our separate ways, it is not good. We are left deprived of the peace and the affirmation that flows from healthy relationships. This deprivation can restrain His flow of life-giving creativity and can cause stagnation in our lives. It can cause our future to literally be put on pause, and it can even cause our physical bodies to suffer. But God is a God of hope and restoration, and He has provided the way home for us.

Our Father's love for us is a practical love. He is not far removed from our complicated lives. He is near to us and committed to providing everything we need in order for our lives to work and be fruitful. He knew that we would hurt each other, and so He has wisely supplied our recourse for when relationships fall apart. It is our only recourse. In the event that it does not appeal to you, there really is no other option. We must forgive. He has given us His example to follow and requires us to do likewise. Refusing to forgive will keep you trapped. It will poison your heart and slowly seep its way into every area of your life. Forgiving is costly, but without it you will never move forward.

Where is another God like you, who pardons the sins of … his people? You cannot stay angry with your people, for you love to be merciful. Once again you will have compassion on us. You will tread our sins beneath your feet; you will throw them into the depths of the ocean![6] God's grace looks for sin and gets excited about forgiving it. It is who He is. It is what He does. It is why He came. Forgiving is what He does best.

Our Father does not just obsess over His rules.
God has never been soft on sin—
but He has always been so high on
mercy that it looks that way.
—JOHNNY ENLOW

Jesus tells a story in the Bible simply because He wants us to understand this incredible heart of mercy that beats within our Father.[7] He tells a story about a sheep that wanders away from the fold. Now we don't know if this sheep was a sweet, little fellow with adorably crooked ears, and yet just enough mischievous wanderlust that it headed out looking for greener pastures. Or maybe it really was a big, nasty, smelly old sheep that was always biting and kicking its companions in the pen. None of this seemed to matter to the Father. All that mattered to Him was that the sheep was missing, separated from family, and without protection and proper food. So He left all the other sheep and went after this lost one, and He searched until He found it. The wayward sheep saw the Father coming and was undone by His love to pursue him in this faraway country, and it fell into His arms. The Father then put it over His sturdy shoulders and joyfully brought it home. The sweet aroma and sound of undeserved restoration and reconciliation reverberated in Heaven, and the great cloud of witnesses leaned out over the balcony to listen and see. A party broke out, and all the angels danced.

Is it possible that you could go after those who have bitten and kicked you ... those who have recklessly pierced your heart and then shamelessly wandered away to greener pastures? They messed up their own life and then they messed up yours too. They deeply hurt you. What if your heart and your love and your hope risked going after them? What if you picked them up and put them on your shoulders through your prayers for them? What if you began to think about them differently and talk about them differently?

What if Jesus really wants to use you to bring them home? Forgiveness. It is the most powerful force in creation.

our Obedience

We must allow our hearts to come forward. We are learning to live our life with our heart fully engaged, and we must make room for it to have place. We cannot drive a car without engaging the ignition. Likewise, if we aspire to effectively occupy the driver's seat of our own life, we need to understand that we cannot do that without engaging our heart. We have to guard our hearts closely, because all the issues of life flow from the heart.[8] The heart is the origin of all fruitfulness. It is the ignition; it ignites and brings fire to everything we put our hand to.

It is in the heart that forgiveness is conceived. The Lord invites us and empowers us to forgive. Many years ago, I received the following prophetic word:

> *So you can forgive and release those who spitefully have used you, even those who took from your life, even emotional robbery, because when you have something from God, you can't be robbed.*

During the long healing process of our family, the Lord regularly spoke to me through dreams in the night. One of those dreams came just after my husband and I had relocated to a different state. It was a dream about our sons, and it was a dream about forgiveness. It was my first dream in our new home, and from the dream I understood that this home was going to play a part in the restoration of our family. In the dream I was covering our sons with piles and piles of cotton balls. These cotton balls were soaked and drenched in the blood of Jesus. I was gathering them, as many as I could hold in my arms, and piling them on our sons. Then, in the dream, I heard the words, "Saving blood, mercy and grace, saving blood, mercy and grace." Then there was a strong impartation of the power of the blood of Christ to redeem all sinners and the zeal of His love to do so.

This was a dream of comfort for me, and it was also a dream of instruction. God was letting me know that regardless of all that might yet lie ahead, there was abundant redemption available for our sons. The Lord knows that forgiveness can actually leave us shaken at times, and He never asks us to forgive that He does not provide the grace for it. An abundance of forgiveness was going to be needed, but the Lord was asking us to keep piling on the cotton balls. The blood of Jesus would cover it. There was even a humorous twist to this dream. Our family name is Johnson, and the cotton balls in the dream were Johnson and Johnson.

> **Jesus never asks us to forgive without giving us the grace for it**

LOVE – *the* CROWN JEWEL

In 1976 a man who greatly loved the Lord became critically ill. His name is Bob Jones, and he is very loved by many. While in his hospital bed, Bob Jones had a death experience in which he was taken to heaven. In his recounting of that experience, Bob says, "I watched the Lord speak to people that were coming there. And He asked them only one question: Did you learn to love? He's not going to ask you what you did. If you learn to love, you are going to do that which is right. Did you learn to love? He would ask them that question and they would say, Yes Lord, and He would kiss them right on the lips and embrace them, and the double doors of His heart would open and they would go right on in."[9]

None of us were ever really asked, but on the day we were born we were automatically enrolled in the School of Love. We all get intentionally assigned to different schools; nevertheless, it is the same School. Our classmates are hand-picked for us, and our curriculums are individually designed. Dropping out is always an option, but no matter how far we run, some of the classmates will be around forever and the test we never took will simply follow us. Did you learn to love?

It can be easy to over assess our capacity to love unless and until life suddenly catapults us beyond the pressure point where our own love has previously been able to sustain us.

That is when we know that the Lord is very tenderly watching over us, because He knows we are being stretched. Our Teacher, the Holy Spirit, is administering a test. He believes in us, and He wants to take us into new territory. He wants to promote us to a higher place where He knows we will not survive unless our love experiences an upgrade.

In 2001 these words were prophesied over me:

> *And that's what God is causing in your heart. There's gonna be a compassion that's gonna rise up and you're gonna begin to minister and intercede for some of those very difficult cases. Those whom even pastors don't want to be challenged with. But it's gonna require a change on the inside. And this change will be perpetual. It's not meant to hurt. It's meant to strengthen. It's meant to exhibit the very nature of Christ ... you will be a living testimony in the nature of Jesus with the compassion that he puts in your heart.*

He comes to change us on the inside. And although it may hurt, it causes us to grow strong.

We cannot give what we do not have. Many of us arrive in the land of adulthood extremely love deprived and full of bullet holes. We need to get our tank filled up. Once we have a fresh flow of love coming in, then we have love to give away. That is the

We cannot give what we do not have

only way it works. We are not supermen. We must get the love first from somewhere before we can give it away. This is our birthright in God. Our greatest responsibility every day is to receive our Father's love. We must receive it afresh every day. We beat ourselves up so badly until we truly step into that place of friendship with Him where His love washes us clean every moment, and at last we understand our worth. Read again how the Lord supplied love for me to give to my mom when I had none. He simply showed me to make a withdrawal from the love that I had received from Him. Allow the Lord to lavish His love upon you. Make these words your own testimony for whatever you are facing.

> All of a sudden, right there in the van, the words of John shot up from deep within me. *My command is this: Love each other as I have loved you.*[10] As I have loved you … as I have loved you … as I have loved you. The words rolled over and over in my mind like a powerful cascading waterfall. They were charged with electricity as my spirit man rose up to lay hold of the revelation. The Lord was not asking me to love my mother the way that He loved her. He was asking me to love her **as He had loved me.**
>
> It was profound. Absolutely profound! Yes, yes! Oh, yes, yes! That was a love I knew. Oh, how I knew that love! That was the love that had brought me up out of darkness. That was the love that had carried me

when I could not put one foot in front of another. When I had cried out for the grave, when the well within me had run bone dry, when the hurt and the pain had caused me to lash out against an unseen enemy, that was the love that had put a song in my heart and taught my feet to dance. That was the love, oh, that was the love that had made me whole again. Tears streamed down my face, and my heart began to overflow with brokenness. I knew I could give that love to my mother.

That was the love that had the power to heal both of us.

the INVITATION

It is not possible to stray beyond the reach of Heaven's love. The particulars of how we may have wandered from the fold are of no consequence to Jesus. He will always come after us. At the right time, and in the right way, He will begin to require more of us. But for now, He simply comes to carry us home. He has done that for me. I know what it feels like to stand in need of forgiveness. Years after giving my heart to Him, the Lord very pointedly brought to the surface a transgression from my past. Although I had worked through that all privately with Him, I knew that He was requiring me to go to those involved and seek their forgiveness. It was a very, very painful time as I dealt with shame and the searing accusations of those I had hurt and who still carried the scars.

The Lord is inviting you to allow him to wipe your slate clean. Forgiveness can seem so overwhelming sometimes that we wonder, why bother? But as the years went by, and I moved forward into the future and into God's call on my life, I often cried at the goodness of the Father to have so graciously closed that door in my life. Those relationships were now healed, and through the forgiveness that others extended to me, the enemy could never again dredge that up. God wants to close the doors in your past. You are moving into your driver's seat, and as you journey along your highway , you must never be afraid of the scene in your rearview mirror.

So this is a time to receive His cleanness and His peace. It is a time for wounds to be forgiven and washed away, for your own self first and then for others … old wounds and fresh wounds … wounds that others have inflicted upon you and wounds that you have inflicted upon others. Many times the two will be intertwined. You do not need to be anxious; you do not need to try to force anything. You only need to present yourself and let His gentle love lead the way. The Lord will then take you by the hand and walk you through this. Stay alert and stay sensitive. When eruptions break out, know that the Holy Spirit is at work, just like what happened at my mom's cottage. Rejoice, because that is the Lord putting His finger on a place that He wants to heal.

CONCLUSION

The Lord is passionate about our relationships and stands ready always to heal. He teaches us how to fight, He fights alongside us, and He fights for us. For some of you, there has always been an inward struggle. There has always been a battle over the issue of love. You have felt an emptiness. You have felt a void … a gap. You have always really wanted to know the love of God in a greater way. You have sometimes found people overbearing as they have come at you with harsh words. Even when you have done all you knew to do, it did not seem to be enough.

God is going to move upon your heart and heal you in many different ways, even ways you did not know you needed healing. As the Lord has looked down upon you, there have been tears from heaven. Where things of your memory have haunted you, the Lord is going to wash away your pain. There are things He will be pruning from you, and there are things He will be instilling in you. If there is any major, any minor, bit of hate that would cause you to begin to feel as though you need to come against anything or anyone, He is going to heal that.

Love will always bring those near and give to you the blessings that He so desires for you to have. You are going to be securely rooted and grounded in this transforming love, and you will know the joy of giving that love away. You will have forgiveness to give away. Love and forgiveness are inseparably tied together. There will be a perpetual change on the inside of you that will become a wellspring of strength for you. Your heart will become fully engaged and you will love with the love by which you have been loved.

PRAYER

Father, praise You and thank You for who You are. When our lives are broken, You fix them. You are not worried and You are not angry. All things are possible with You, Lord. So right now I bring my family to You, the people You have given me to love. I bring the people I work with and even people from my past. Lord, You see every relationship that is broken and everything that is not right. But I am asking You to make these things right again. I ask You to forgive me for the mistakes I have made and for when I have been selfish and have withheld love from those around me. I let go of all the records of wrongs that I have kept against others, and I forgive and release those who have hurt me and used me. I bless them right now to experience Your love and Your peace. Draw us all to Your heart and heal us, Father. Give me dreams in the night that will bring wisdom and direction for me. Remove everything that has kept us connected to the flow of pain and restore us, I pray. Amen

THOUGHTS for REFLECTION and DISCUSSION

1. Do you sense the Holy Spirit wanting to bring healing to you in an area of your own life where you need forgiveness?
2. Is there someone you love that you are estranged from?
   - How is that estrangement affecting your peace?
   - Is it affecting your health?
3. In what way is the Lord leading you to allow your heart to come forward in the relationship above?
4. Can you identify words of blessing that a parent has spoken over you?
   - How do those words make you feel about yourself?
   - What have those words activated in your life?
   - Note: A parent's blessing can come in very simple ways. Perhaps your dad always told you that you make him laugh. That is a spoken blessing over your life. It means that you have a gift to refresh people with laughter. Use it!
5. Share about a test that you have gone through and passed in the School of Love.

Endnotes

1. 1 Corinthians 13:9, NIV.
2. John 15:12, NIV.
3. Malachi 4:5-6, NIV.
4. Genesis 27:34, NIV.
5. Hosea 11:3-4, NIV.
6. Micah 7:18-19, TLB.
7. Luke 15:3-7.
8. Proverbs 4:23, NIV.
9. Bob Jones. "Prophecy Still Stirs Many," ©2006 *Charisma News* 3-1-2014.
10. John 15:12, NIV.

Part Three

TAKING THE DRIVER'S SEAT

*A man's gift makes room for him
and brings him before the great.*
—PROVERBS 18:16, ESV

Chapter Five

Living in Confident Boldness

FREEDOM to REMOVE the COAT

The last worship song was ending, and our afternoon speaker was getting her notes together and heading to the podium. I had been up front dancing for quite a long time … a very beautiful and wild tribal dance with a rhythmic stomping, and I was feeling exuberant and out of breath as I returned to my seat. I was sitting in the front row, and the speaker picked up the microphone, turned, and asked me to come forward. "Ma'am, can I pray for you before I start?"

She then began to share her heart. "The Lord gave me a word for you. And He said that you are willing to be undignified if need be. That people look at you and they see dignity and class. But the Lord says that you are willing to lay down your dignity and class if need be to do whatever He has asked you to do. And He said, in that place of humility, is the exact place that He uses to minister to others. And He said He uses that same place in your heart to minister to you. He tells me that it is in that place of worship, of dancing before Him, where you just get undignified, He says there lies your victory over all things. That is what has kept you, and that is what's gonna continue to keep you, is that place where you can just get down and dirty with the Lord so to speak."

In the first chapter of the book, I shared my dream of flying on the Titanic. I shared the following words about the last thing that took place in that dream:

> As I continued flying, I became aware that I had on a heavy, cumbersome winter coat. I was having the time of my life flying, but I knew that I could fly better without the coat. So I took the coat off. I just boldly took it off. When I did, I laughed out loud again, because I discovered that I was flying in a bikini! Then the dream ended.

Later in the chapter I shared this:

> Finally, the fourth spiritual treasure that we encounter in the dream is that flying represents a heart that

is totally abandoned to boldly embracing its own uniqueness. It cares not if no one else in the room is flying. It has learned long ago how to be happy enough to fly solo when needed. This entire focus of confident, personal freedom is sharply portrayed through the spontaneous shedding of the heavy, winter coat. As we journey through life, we accumulate all sorts of outer garments that serve to protect us from being fully known, even to ourselves. These garments will need to be removed in order to facilitate ease of flight and to accommodate promotion to higher levels. In contrast to the weighted coat, the surprise bikini portrays a light-hearted abandonment and a transparency that permits others to see more of the real you. It speaks of an absence of self-consciousness and self-awareness and of an agenda that has nothing to hide. It represents the substance of child-like innocence.

> *Actually, there must be a total abandonment of anything that limits your ability to be yourself. Otherwise, you will spend your life dreaming about the greatness of others, instead of living out your own authentic existence.*
> —LARRY RANDOLPH, *Original Breath*

In a very real sense, you have to come to the place where you are free enough to remove the heavy winter coat. The speaker had said to me, "But the Lord says that you are willing to lay down your dignity and class if need be to do whatever He has asked you to do." She said that that was the exact place from which ministry flowed, both to my own heart and to others, and she said that that was the place of all my victory. Dignity is a type of coat.[1] Dignity is not something that on its own is good or bad. It is simply that it is something that can hinder us if we are not free to step out of it when needed.

The Holy Spirit wants our hearts to be free. He is continually inviting us into greater and greater personal freedoms of the heart. Although I knew well how to wear this coat and how to carry myself with dignity, at the same time I was free enough to remove the coat if needed. And the bold, disarming removal of it released an expression of abandonment and transparency that arrested hearts. People were touched, because the human heart recognizes true freedom and is captivated by it. In the dream, my own heart recognized and took flight through my expression of freedom.

INTENTIONAL MAKEOVER

Our journey is more than reaching a destination. It is about how we travel and who and what we become on the way. In the early years, I received a prophetic word that included these words: "I'm gonna cause you to have great courage and boldness. I'm setting you free with knowing Me. The more that you know Me, the more bold that you will become. Within you there is gonna be a boldness that you've never known before. There's gonna be a confidence. I'm placing within you a confidence in who you are and who I've called you to be."

By faith, I took these words to heart. I was attracted to boldness, and I wanted the demonstration of boldness in my life. I identified three attributes that I knew needed to be solidly established in my life in order for me to bring my inner man to a place that would be conducive to boldness. I grabbed onto the promise of future boldness, while at the same time I began to focus on building a strong foundation marked by confidence, security, and stability. It was a huge undertaking, but I wanted it with all my heart, and I knew these areas of my life were shaky.

I wrote out simple definitions of these three words in my journal:

- Confidence is assurance and belief in one's own abilities.
- Security is freedom from fear and anxiety and a sense of safety.
- Stability is the capacity of an object to return to its original position after having been displaced; it is the absence of double-mindedness or being of two minds.

I memorized these definitions and returned to them consistently for years. This caused me to know quickly when I was off course so that I could intentionally recalibrate. Over time, my inner core of self-identity underwent significant transformation, until I rarely needed to think about it or go back to the definitions.

I literally re-trained my responses in these areas. When I would begin to believe that I could not do something well, or that I could not think well or make good choices, I would tenaciously choose confidence in its place, believe in myself and step into it. When I would begin to feel alone, or unprotected, unworthy in some way or guilty in some way, I would deliberately set my mind upon the Lord's delight in me and the safety of His love, and I would feel secure, clean and empowered.

When suddenly I would find wrong emotions beginning to take charge of me, such as anger or self-pity, I almost instantly would be on alert. Even though at times I would still press full speed ahead into indulging those emotions, that became harder and harder to do as the desire to walk in stability grew stronger and stronger within me. This is probably the area that most significantly redefined me. I reached a point where I outright refused double-mindedness and began to walk in unshakeable confidence. Over and over again, I demanded of myself to embrace stability and develop the capacity within myself to quickly return to my original identity in Christ.

This change, predominately internal at first, completely altered the way that I perceived myself and carried myself. Through it all, an authentic boldness was being quietly established within me. We are not talking about a type of arrogant boldness that manifests itself as rebellion. We are talking about an inward, Godly confidence and fearlessness that empowers one to become all they were designed to be. We are speaking of the freedom and conviction to take risks and to move in bold demonstrations of love and faith.

We are talking about a full stretching out of the heart that overshadows all self-awareness. You have stepped into a place where you thought you could never go ... a place where the air is crisp and clear, where compromise does not exist and where your words and your actions come forth from your innermost being because your heart is fully alive. There has to be a boldness that is bold enough to confront and disarm the boldness of our enemy. Even in your personal battle to change and move forward, even in something as simple as extending forgiveness, you are going to face off with your own resistance. It will only be conquered through bold tenacity.

> **Even in something as simple as extending forgiveness, you are going to face off with your own resistance**

There needs to be bold love, bold faith, bold worship, bold prayer and bold rejoicing. In Scripture, the Greek word *parresia* is used as a blend for both confidence and boldness. It means freedom in speaking all that one thinks, deeds which imply a special exercise of faith, and confident praying and witnessing. The righteous are as bold as a lion.[2] The Hebrew word *batah*, translated in this verse as bold, is the word for trust. Boldness is a reflection of firm, unshakable trust in God. Trust and boldness walk hand in hand.

Removing the coat is symbolic of bold freedom. Removing the coat was the last thing that took place in the dream, which indicates that there is a progression that leads to boldness. You will recognize the progression as you journey through it. First, you were captivated with the thought of flying, and your heart said, "I believe in that! I want that!" With time, you mastered the art of flying solo, all the while still loving and honoring those traveling on the ship with you, but who have no interest in flying. Wow, that part was hard! You began to exchange the lies in your heart for truth, erecting solid places, high places, from which you could consistently take flight. Then, people began noticing. Suddenly, you began bubbling over with your story and slowly it dawns on you … the Lord is awarding you your flight instructor's license and you are teaching others to fly. You are already removing the coat, you know it, and you are giddy.

It is insightful that in the dream the coat was removed as I was teaching others how to fly. This is another spiritual truth, that as you begin to give away to others what you have learned, your confidence begins to grow quickly. You are making decisions, and you are enlarging others through the giving away of your own life. You are in the driver's seat and you are living life with your heart fully engaged. It was a very special day for me, years later, when these words were confirmed over me:

> *But the Lord would say you're bold, you're brazen, you're unapologetic. You got guts, girl. And the Lord would say, you got guts. You got guts. You got guts. I want you to stand by what I told you to do.*

Father always rewards our faithfulness.

AFRAID of NOTHING

We have to begin to think differently. Our lives are changed when we think differently.[3] We need a new filter, a new mindset, for hearing God and for interpreting His voice to us. We must change our focus. The Lord is lifting your eyes off of your circumstances and repositioning your focus upon that which lives inside you. He wants you to know who you are. He wants you to know who He made you to be. He wants you to align yourself with where He is taking you. He wants you to know what your assignment is. You were made for a holy purpose, and He is going to walk with you as you grow to own and develop that purpose. As you boldly set your face toward seeking for understanding, the Lord is going to begin to give you insight into the dream that He put inside you.

Years ago, I was sitting up in the late night hours reading my Bible. I was curled up all comfy on the sofa with a little table lamp next to me, when suddenly the passage I was reading from seemed to come alive in neon lighting. I felt the words leap off the page and wrap themselves around me. I sat quietly for a time, totally arrested, and then I read the passage again. Then I read through it again as I began to slowly comprehend what was happening. The Holy Spirit came over me, and I heard the Lord saying: *This is who you are. This is who I made you to be. And I will see to it that you become it.* It was as if I could feel a mantle come down upon me, granting enormous security, validation and permission.

> *Do you give the horse his strength*
> *or clothe his neck with a flowing mane?*
> *Do you make him leap like a locust,*
> *striking terror with his proud snorting?*
> *He paws fiercely, rejoicing in his strength,*
> *and charges into the fray.*
> *He laughs at fear, afraid of nothing;*
> *he does not shy away from the sword.*
> *The quiver rattles against his side,*
> *along with the flashing spear and lance.*
> *In frenzied excitement he eats up the ground;*

he cannot stand still when the trumpet sounds.
At the blast of the trumpet he snorts, "Aha!"
He catches the scent of battle from afar,
the shout of commanders and the battle cry.[4]

Heaven was naming me. The Father was saying that when He looks at me, this is what He sees. When He formed me in my mother's womb, this is who He made me to be. But it was more than that. He was giving me this passage for others. He was showing me that this horse is a picture of how He sees His end-time Bride. She is a warrior bride fashioned to be at His side. The Lord has made her strong. Clothed in her Bridegroom's love, she is innocently disconcerting, causing great confusion in the enemy's camp. She throws back her head and snorts proudly as she strikes terror in their hearts. She is fiercely overjoyed by her strength and charges into the fray. She laughs at fear, afraid of nothing. This babe is bold!

She does not shy away from the sword as her weapons rattle and flash at her side. Her heart is aflame with a desire to advance God's Kingdom and glory over any rival. Upon the blasting of the trumpet, the far-away scent of battle, the shout of commanders and the battle cry, the heart and spirit of the Lord's true end-time Bride will be fully revealed for all to see. In the same spirit as this warrior horse, she will no longer be relied upon to remain faithful to the parameters of men to keep her in place. She was made for war, and she cannot stand still when the trumpet sounds.

Permission is granted to snort, "Aha!" The next time you are overwhelmed, discouraged, or cannot see the way forward, remember who you are. Rejoice in your strength. The enemy is terrified of you, and you do not have to be afraid of anything. You were made for war.

random CAR DREAM LESSONS

I have a steady history of dreams that revolve around my car. These dreams are a lot of fun, sometimes even humorous, and God uses them consistently in my life to give me understanding and direction. In the past, He has used them as progress markers during my journey to get into the driver's seat, bringing clarity to things otherwise hidden. And now that I am in my own driver's seat, He continues to use them to provide direction. Enjoy this sampling of dreams and allow the Lord to bring you wisdom and understanding through them.

Flaming Swords

Dream: My very first dream involving my car was a long time ago. In the dream it was nighttime, and my car was parked off to the side in the dark. There were two people in the dream. They were wearing masks of goodness, but they were actually evil and they were intent on killing me. I knew that through their evil powers they had caused my car to stop running. They fought against me with flaming swords, but I overcame them with the name of Jesus. Then suddenly, in the dream, it was daylight, and I began vibrantly dancing and praising and shouting.

Interpretation: This is a spiritual warfare dream. As we set our heart upon walking out this thing, there will be battles to fight. Darkness will withstand you in your journey. People, even people who appear good, will seek to harm you and prevent you from reaching your destination. But your victory in Jesus is certain.

Abandoned Cars

Dream: I dreamed I had gone to my pastor's home. Their home was situated on a dry, dusty spread out property. When I came back outside to leave, I was not able to locate my car. Suddenly I saw that there were cars everywhere I looked, in all directions on the property, all in various stages of abandonment. I wandered around for a long time, and at last I saw my car at the bottom of a steep hill.

Interpretation: This is a wisdom dream. Ultimately, we are responsible to own and develop our own call and destiny. We cannot abdicate that to our church leaders. Some churches are dry and dusty and the callings upon the people lie abandoned and unactivated.

Serving Others

Dream: I dreamed that some important people put their belongings in my car so that I could transport them to the next place. I drove my car into an underground parking garage and parked it, and the people came and got their things out of my car. They never spoke or acknowledged me. My eyes fastened upon a stunning pair of silver-metallic, jewel-encrusted slacks lying in the back seat, and I watched as a beautiful young woman took them.

Interpretation: This is a dream to bring understanding. This dream could interpret differently depending on the circumstances of the dreamer. At the time, I understood exactly what the Holy Spirit was speaking to me. Suppose this was your dream. Do you feel your life is all about running around serving other people who never acknowledge or thank you? Perhaps these people even have callings that you admire. Invite the Lord right now to speak personally to your heart through this dream.

Torn Gown

Dream: I was in a vehicle on my way to a very exciting, important event. The vehicle was under my authority, yet I was not in the driver's seat. I was in the passenger seat next to the door. We had been traveling for a while when we entered the city environment where the important event was being held. It was a beautiful and strategic, high-energy city. The man driving began to look for a parking space. I kept seeing several good ones, but he passed them all by. Suddenly I looked around inside the car and realized that it was jam-packed front and back. I exclaimed, "Oh my! There's seventeen of us in here!" Because it was now late, the man driving the vehicle pulled over, and all the people jumped out and started up the hill to the stately, stone building where the event was being held. They knocked me down and walked over me as I lay on the ground next to the car door. I saw that I had been dressed in a beautiful, shimmery gown, but it had been torn off me and was lying beside me. I gathered myself and crawled into the driver's seat. It was getting dark and I knew I had to get some clothes on. Suddenly my infant grandson appeared in the back seat, and I knew the best thing was to get back home where there would be food and a bottle for him when he woke up.

Interpretation: This is a dream of comfort. There is a beautiful, exciting and strategic place that God is taking us to. We are dressed and eager to be there. But there are a lot of other people in our life. At the time of this dream, there were exactly seventeen in mine! Those of our own family may not always value our spiritual journey. They may walk right over top of us in their pursuit of their own agenda, knocking us down and *taking away our clothes*.[5] God wants to comfort us. He sees exactly where we are and He cares. He is with us, and with our hand in His hand, we are learning to love. In our heart, we already live in the shining city, and in due time, we will be openly rewarded.

Turn Left!

Dream: I dreamed there was some sort of continuous ride that many of us had been on for a long time. I was in the front car of this ride which was an open sort of thing like at an amusement park. There were many others in the open cars that were attached behind me. We started climbing and suddenly going up, up, up, coming up out of thick, rich green, jungle-like foliage. Suddenly we peaked, and I shouted in delight, "We're on a roller coaster!" We started going down, down, fast, fast, again flying through thick, gorgeous green foliage. It was exhilarating. Then suddenly there was no track beneath us, and our cars were flying along through the jungle on a worn and packed down dirt path. Somehow my ride ended, and I found myself standing inside a small, cement changing facility. None of the other roller coaster cars had arrived yet. I changed my clothes, and I tried to open the door to go out, but I remember not feeling sure if I should do that. My husband and those I loved were still out there in the cars that had been far behind me. Should I wait for them? It is like I kept looking for someone in authority to give me permission to open the door and go out. Then I was just suddenly there, outside the changing facility that marked the end of the long journey. I was in my car coming out of a parking area, and I was driving over to the door to wait for my husband. But all at once Johnny Enlow, a well-known prophet, was right in front of me directing traffic from his car. He rolled down his window, and with his finger he directed me to turn left and form a line to leave the area. That would make me the first in line. I was sure that I should go over to the door of the changing facility and wait for my husband. Johnny knew that I was wrestling with indecision, and he looked directly at me with stern apostolic authority and mild irritation that I might disobey the Lord. My car was brown, and Johnny was dressed in all brown in a brown car.

Interpretation: This is a calling dream. Permission is granted to move forward. This dream is a dream of permission and a strong wake-up call to move forward. Loyalty can make us feel that we must wait on those we love and not go on without them. But each of the Father's children has their own private launch. It is not a group thing. The color brown speaks of humility. The Lord eventually brings us to the end of the wild ride, and He sends us forth in the fresh clothes of humility.

Red Light

Dream: I was sitting in my car stopped at an intersection. It was morning and the sun was shining. There were beautiful trees in every direction and no other cars in sight. It was very still. The signal light was bright red. The light stayed red. And it stayed red. And it stayed red. I felt peaceful. Then suddenly I realized my car had stopped running. I felt I should start it in case the light turned green. But when I reached for the ignition, I discovered that my keys were gone.

Interpretation: This is a direction dream. The red light means stop. God has shut down the old season, we are facing new direction and we must be still and wait for new keys. When the Lord is leading us in a new direction that He knows is going to feel strange to us, even causing us to be unsure, He will speak very clearly. He is a good leader. The light is always green unless He speaks otherwise.

Kind Chauffeur

Dream: In this dream, I was in a chauffeured car of some sort, well built and strong. It was driven by a very kind, unassuming man who was wearing a cab driver's hat. I was in the front passenger seat. We were just starting out on our trip, and as I leaned up against my door, I was aware that it was not securely closed. I tried several times to close it, but I did not have the strength. The driver was very compassionate and gentle in his concern that I get it closed. Finally my arm was strong enough to latch the door securely. I felt the kindness of the driver so strongly, and it meant so much to me.

Interpretation: This is a dream of affirmation. Eventually, as we pass through our tests and our training, the gentle kindness of the Holy Spirit will supply the strength we need to securely close every door to our past, every door of unforgiveness, and every door that would hold us back. Then He will put on His cab driver's hat, and He Himself will take the driver's seat of our life.

the INVITATION

There is a wonderfully new version of you that is straining to burst forth from the gate. You possess a unique style of boldness, a power inside you that is groaning to be expressed. God knows that you are far better than you know. Some of you have felt like your real voice has not been heard in a long time and have wondered where it has gone. May I just be really bold? Throw off what others have put on you. Stop apologizing for who you are and who you are not. Stop yearning to explain everything that you have thought was wrong about you. Trust your instincts. Go buy a new outfit. Get a new hairstyle. Sing out loud. Sing your favorite song. Ask yourself why it is your favorite. Why that song? What is that song saying that resonates with you? Own that song! Dance to that song! Shout! Laugh until your stomach hurts! Stick a geranium in your hat and be happy! The Lord Jesus is enlarging your territory. It is your coronation day.

> **There is a wonderful new version of you that is straining to burst forth from the gate**

> *I have spent a lot of time in my life being a people pleaser! Never getting to say and do things that express who I am as an individual and a lady in Christ. I WILL NOT conform any more!!! Don't try to make me feel bad or encourage me to be someone other than who God created me to be! I do the things and say the things I do for a reason!*
>
> —JESSICA MARIE

CONCLUSION

Jesus talked to trees,[6] and Jesus invites us to talk to mountains.[7] He even tells us what to say to the mountains. Our lives are meant to be a great adventure. We must allow God to promote us to where He wants to take us. He came to give us fullness of life, life that is more than enough, so that we will always have an overflow to give away. We absolutely cannot fail when we partner with Him. He breaks the power of fear that wars against us. Ferociously He scales our Mount Everest and hoists our flag of victory. Then He calls out valiantly to us from atop the hill of our future and beckons our revived hearts to believe once more.

He calls out valiantly to us from atop the hill of our future and beckons our revived hearts to believe once more

Fear will blind our vision. But as we walk in faith that He is with us, we will always see the way to go. Less and less we will trust in our self, and more and more we will boldly put our confidence in Him.

> *He places His desires for your created purpose within your heart and then creates a life to fulfill them.*
> —CINDY MCGILL

PRAYER

Father, thank You that I am so special to You. Thank You for your kindness toward me. I love You, Lord, and I really do hear Your voice calling me. I hear You calling me to come out further to a place where the waters are deeper and stronger. I feel You even motioning me, and giving me permission, to go ahead of the others who are around me. Lord, do Your work in me to tear down the fences and the boundaries that I have erected around myself, and cause me to see the vastness and largeness of the plans that are in Your heart concerning my life. I choose to go there with You, Lord. I celebrate who You have made me to be, I rejoice in my strength, and I confidently and boldly set out with You on this adventure of living in confident boldness, leaning into You, afraid of nothing.

THOUGHTS for REFLECTION and DISCUSSION

1. What comes to mind for you when you reflect on living out your own authentic existence?
2. What upgrades do you anticipate for yourself in the areas of confidence, security and stability?
3. Do you have a scripture verse or passage that has leaped off the page and wrapped itself around you? Maybe it was a still small voice that called your name as you were reading. Share what that has spoken to you.
4. Which dream in particular spoke to your situation and how? What action do you need to take?

Endnotes

1. 2 Samuel 6:20-22, NIV.
2. Proverbs 28:1, NIV.
3. Romans 12:2, NIV.
4. Job 39:19-25, NIV.
5. Song of Songs 5:7, NIV.
6. Mark 11:14,20, NIV.
7. Mark 11:20-25, NIV.

Chapter Six

Setting the Banquet Table

NEW BEGINNINGS
hope DEFERRED

Hope deferred makes the heart sick, but a longing fulfilled is a tree of life.[1] The journey from hope deferred to longing fulfilled, the journey from sickness of heart to a tree of life, can often try our faith. As time passed during those early years of my journey, the sound of laughter grew fainter and fainter, until slowly the song of hope within me grew silent. It was replaced by a deafening scream of abandonment. Shame paralyzed me and icy fear numbed me. The years of relentless darkness had shattered all my man-made doctrines and left me exhausted. As I have shared earlier, I came to a place where I did not want to go on, and my tormented spirit cried out to die. God heard my cry and revived me.

Twenty more years went by with no change. For a long time, I had known in my spirit that my mother's death was going to mark the beginning of a new and significant season in my life. Fifty days after her passing, my husband, Hollis, received a sudden and unusual promotion. We were on the threshold of retirement, and this new assignment would require us to uproot and relocate to another state. It was a very wrenching time for us as we contended for direction and the right decision. That summer we left Ohio believing we were following the voice of God. We went by faith, and faith alone, not knowing where we were going.[2] We left behind our daughter, most of our grandchildren, and our two sons who were deep in heroin addiction. In our hearts we felt we had abandoned them all and we agonized deeply.

Life was hard in the new location. Hollis was hospitalized five times for serious kidney stones and struggled to regain his strength. I was called to Colorado for four months to care for our middle daughter and grandson who were in a violent car accident and were not expected to live. News came that both our sons had been imprisoned again. Everything looked like hope deferred. Yet deep in my spirit, somehow I knew we were on the right path. I could smell fresh air just around the corner, and *against all hope, in hope I believed.*[3]

longing FULFILLED

In the early spring of that next year, all our goods were loaded onto the moving van once again. Only nine months after moving us in, the large truck pulled out slowly from the driveway of our rental home in Chicago. At the bottom of the hill, it made the wide turn and headed south for Tennessee. During those nine months, we had made trips to several states in search of our retirement future. And now once more, by faith, and faith alone, we headed out. The Lord honored my husband's forty year career with a financial gift that would never have transpired if we had not followed Him into the new place. And He sent us out with our wagons full. As we barreled down the highway, the destination on our GPS read Tennessee. But although we did not know it yet, it read quite differently in Heaven. In heaven our destination read: **Longing Fulfilled.**

Our new home was situated in the mountains. It was quiet and tucked back in on the water … a place far removed from the past … a place where new beginnings could germinate and new vision could be birthed and established. We spent the summer making the home and property ours, cleaning and mending and painting and planting.

In the fall we returned to Ohio to visit our daughter. While we were there, one of our sons got word to us and asked if he could come back to Tennessee to live with us. We drove to the run-down place where he was living, near a truck stop on the edge of town. He did not come out of the dark motel room, and we quickly realized he was too sick on heroin for us to take him with us. We bought him groceries, paid his motel charge for the month, and once again entrusted him to Heaven's love. But his twin brother was also there with him. We had not seen him in almost three years, and he stepped outside their room onto the hot, sunlit macadam and talked with us. He was very broken. As our visit ended and we said goodbye, he seemed to be struggling. Late that evening, at our daughter's, we began packing up our bags to return to Tennessee. Suddenly an unknown text came in and it was him. "Could I come home with you? I can be ready whatever time you say." I showed it to our daughter and she cried. In our hearts, we knew it was the Lord.

In the early morning darkness, we picked up our son at the door of the seedy motel room in the middle of a cornfield. He rode the entire eight-hour trip in the back seat. It was years since he had possessed a driver's license ... uh, legal that is! All his earthly belongings, including a very worn out pillow, sat in the rear of the car in four black garbage bags. It felt like we had kidnapped someone and were transporting human cargo across state lines. He left behind a city-wide police force that had known him and watched his every move for over twenty years. Now it was his dad and me watching as he sat under the trees with his early morning coffee, drinking in the mountain air and staking his new claim on life. Five weeks later we brought his brother home.

It was to save lives that God sent me ahead of you.[4] God had sent us ahead to prepare a place where all the years of pain and heartache and destruction could be restored. Hope deferred had lasted twenty six years. Then, suddenly, the longing was fulfilled and the tree of life took root. Our sons walked clean from all addiction, dead-end hopelessness and suicide. There were still many trips back north for pending court hearings, but our sons stepped out of the enemy's designs and began the journey forward into their destinies.

our LOVE INCUBATOR
Divine Setup

I do not think a single one of us could have fathomed for a moment what we had stepped into. At age twelve, our sons had exited planet Earth, and in all their years that followed, there had never been a normal day. Now they were men who had lived for years on their own. Although the tree of life had taken root, bringing the tree to maturity would prove to be a marathon race of its own. It was a divine setup, and our mission, should we choose to accept it, was redemption.

Once we are walking in freedom, we are sent back to rescue others. God uses our life to set a banqueting table where others can come and eat. When we learn to fly, it is for the purpose of teaching others to fly. My mastery of flight had advanced far enough that the Lord knew He could trust me with this assignment. Nevertheless, I was totally unprepared for the depths of love that I would have to go to in order to stay airborne. Nor did I understand the supply of supernatural wisdom that I was going to need in order to know where the boundaries of that love began and ended.

Who could have ever imagined that the four of us would live together again after all those years? And yet God knew it was the only way to bring us all to wholeness. I found myself calling it our little love incubator, because an incubator is a heated container used for hatching eggs, and it clearly seemed like that was what we were up to. If we could actually get this thing right, the generational cycle of pain and defeat would be forever broken. Our family relationships would step out from the shadows and take their rightful place in the light of the Father's goodness. Blessings that the Lord so desired for us to have, that had been backed up and piled up for years with no way through, would be suddenly released, affecting our family line for generations to come.

It was not going to happen quickly. A prophetic word had been given to me: *"As you will see, I have plans that go far beyond where you have been ... even as the old must pass away, and the new comes walking in with a great Hoorah!"* So the new was going to come *walking in*. It was going to be a steady, step-by-step walk of faithfully placing one foot in front of the other. As deep as the pain and wounding had wedged itself into our hearts, so deep would the love need to go to dislodge it.

It tested us to the core. It was as if each of us had erected a shrine within our heart ... a shrine to the pain that had been inflicted upon us by the others. These individual shrines then melded together, seemingly planting themselves in the middle of our home and creating a memorial to the injustices of the past. Although Hollis and I felt that the Lord had brought our sons there for them to heal and rebuild, we soon realized that they were fully convinced that they were there to heal us. In my heart I knew it was both.

To be honest, we were all surprised by the storm that began to define itself over us. The honeymoon had been beautiful and full of promise, but it faded, and suddenly there was a lot of poison being spewed. Rage and anger were being spewed. Disrespect was rampant. Yet over and over, God said to remain still and simply provide a safe place, a rule-free zone, where the poison could come out. I stood and watched things happening in our home that I knew should not be taking place. Yet, again, the Holy Spirit always restrained me.

I would simply stand in an inner posture of peace. And every time that Hollis or I would feel that we needed to evict them, the other one would not have peace about it.

the FOOLISHNESS of GOD

About a year after they had moved in, I had a dream. In my dream, my husband Hollis was completing some type of test or assignment. He was filling out some paperwork that was required, and he needed my help. I was tired and very angry that we had to keep working on this thing, whatever it was, and I did not want to help. In the dream, I was screaming that we needed to not be doing this stupid thing, and that there were other things we were supposed to be doing with our lives. But Hollis never spoke. I knew that he did not want to be doing it either but was just quietly pressing through it. Then suddenly, there was something he was writing, and I leaned in close because he was not getting it right. In bold, highlighted letters, he was writing *Galatians 2:20*. His hand was shaking as he wrote it, and I put my hand on top of his, and we wrote it together as the dream ended.

When you walk with Jesus, there is a secret language that develops between the two of you. Galatians 2:20 is a code word between the Lord and me. Sometimes when I am traveling, He will put me in room 220. The message is always the same. He is telling me: *This assignment will need to be carried out by faith. Daughter, you will have to put your hand to this thing that is in front of you knowing that your victory will only be secured by faith in Me. Do not be concerned with how you look to others, but trust Me.* Now He was giving us the same message in a dream.

When what we were doing unsettled us, when we were scolded by our other children, when we were judged by friends, when we had nothing but Him, the dream kept our hearts anchored. We never tried to defend ourselves. To others, what we were doing appeared foolish, and often it felt that same way even to us. There were times when shame threatened to swallow us up. Why was it taking so long? What if we had missed the way and were at fault? What if our love had crossed a boundary into deception? Why didn't we just make a list of rules and throw them out if they broke them? What if we were enabling them? Yes, what if we were enabling them? That was the charge that was always brought against us.

And what if we were? Is that the criteria for determining God's will? Does our love end at the place where enabling begins, and will we clearly know where that place is? Is it possible to be obeying God and at the same time be enabling others? Is not the foolishness of God wiser than man's wisdom, and His weakness stronger than man's strength?[5] What if the love incubator was about more than our sons? What if the Lord was relentlessly going after something in us ... something in me? Does not the Lord demand the right to be our only teacher, and must we not find our own revelation from Him?⁶ Must we not come to Him to know our direction, and He will give us what we need to know?

As the months turned into years, and the years began to accumulate, I simply kept on walking by faith just as the Lord had spoken to do. Even in the moments of shame, I had peace, and both the shame and the peace were real at the same time.⁷ The Lord would always send a dream or a prophetic word to encourage me along the way. Here is a part of one of those words that was spoken to me. The Lord makes it very clear that He knows exactly what is taking place, that He is going to bring healing, and that we must wait on His timing:

> *Woe to the obstinate children, to those who carry out plans that are not Mine ... You have done all you know to do. You must wait upon Me now. I will set them free from their sins and death, who now show little respect for you ... your loved ones who have rebelliously turned from you and from Me. The Lord says very clearly He will make a way. His timing is everything. And He shall set it free, each and every one, that you may find yourselves joined together as one ... For if you speak to them too soon about Me or my Father, says the Lord, they will act like pigs and turn on you and hurt you ... Its not always been easy to stand in the light when*

there were those whom you loved who were still in the shadows of darkness ...

a HOPE that DOESN'T LET GO

Then it happened quite unexpectedly. It was always unexpected ... the volatile eruption from out of nowhere. This time though, as we stood quietly watching, Hollis and I both began to feel the same thing. We made the phone call we had thought we would never make again, and in a very short time a police car pulled down our long driveway and two officers in uniform rang our doorbell. We spoke with them for a long time. Our only recourse was to go to the county courthouse and file eviction papers on both our sons. It was late on a Thursday evening, and we made plans to wait until Monday to go. That would give us time to steady our hearts and be fully assured of what we were doing.

I could not sleep that night. The weight on my heart seemed unbearable. We had all invested so much, and I had been unshakably certain that the story would have a happy ending. Is there ever such a thing as throw-away children? Where would they go? Were we going to be severed from them forever? How could it possibly end this way? I prayed for very clear direction.

On Sunday morning, I felt numb and stood quietly through the worship. I surrendered it to Him and knew that we could trust Him with all our heart. At the beginning of the service, Pastor had asked me to read the morning scripture passage. When it came time to go forward after worship, I could barely see through my tears. I found the place and began to read, but quickly Pastor corrected me, "No, I don't think you have the right place." But God knew it was exactly the right place. Pastor then realized that he had written the wrong reference in the bulletin, and he said, "Oh, just go ahead and read what I put there!" So I read out loud what the Lord had known all along that He had wanted me to read, because it was His love-filled direction to us.

I literally sobbed, and my tears dripped onto the pages of my Bible, as I read the words. Jesus was speaking about blessing those who curse you and praying for those who mistreat you. He said to turn the other cheek to those who strike you. He said to not stop those who take from you, to not demand back what they take, and to give without expecting to get anything back because that is what He does. He is kind to the ungrateful and wicked. At the close of the passage, He gives His assurance that even though the floods and torrent may beat against a home and family, the family will stand firm if it is built on the rock of Jesus' words.[8] The Lord was giving clear direction. We knew there would be no trip to the courthouse.

> **We knew there would be no trip to the courthouse**

*He will give us a love for people to the point
that we hope in them and help them put
their crowns on and never take them off
—an indomitable hope
—a hope that doesn't let go or give up on another.*
—BOB HARTLEY

I'LL PAY *for* IT

I dreamed I was in an alterations shop. There was a customer dropping off clothing to be altered, and I was standing off to the side waiting my turn. I was having light conversation with some others when suddenly I heard the customer at the desk say, "I don't have money to pay for that." I turned and looked directly at the woman as though truly seeing her for the first time. Then I said out loud to her, "I'll pay for it."

Setting a banquet table for others is costly. This dream took place in an alterations shop. An alteration is a change or an adjustment to something. The woman in the dream was there with her clothing that no longer fit and needed altered in some way. She represents the harvest field that stands before us. Her life was no longer the right fit. Through varied circumstances, poor choices that were made for her and poor choices that she made for herself, her life had become something other than the life she had dreamed about. She knew this, and she wanted it all to change. She wanted the way she was seen by others to change. She wanted a better fit. So she had gathered her stuff and brought it to a place that promised change, but she soon realized she could not pay the price.

The changing of a life involves emotional investment, time investment and monetary investment. Many of those whom the Father longs to reach in this hour do not have those resources to invest. They cannot make it without help, and the Lord is looking for those who will truly turn their hearts toward the harvest field, see these broken ones and be willing to say, "I'll pay for it!"

When our sons came to live with us, they did not have cars. They did not have driver's licenses. They did not have phones. They did not have checking accounts. They could not get employment because of their criminal records. They owed back court fees and back taxes. They needed critical dental work. They needed education classes. They needed people who would be patient with them. They needed people who were peacemakers. They needed people who would invest the time that love requires.

Almost two years before our sons came to live with us, I received a long prophetic word that ended with the following words:

> *And by the way, there's a financial blessing coming. It's gonna be a big one, a homerun. The works are in the process right now. But God says when it happens,*

> make sure that you remember **your people** financially says the Lord.

Then, less than a year before they came, Hollis received the following word:

> *Hollis, I hear the Spirit of the Lord saying, Son, I'm gonna put it in one hand and then you'll give it, it's like a receiving hand and a giving hand. And when I put in and you receive, you'll transfer and you'll give out. I'm causing you to be a conduit. I'm opening sources to come through you, into you, but not just to remain. I'm not making you a bank, says the Lord, I'm making you a conduit to give and to receive. I'm making you a conduit, in and out, in and out, in and out. And there shall be no end to the supply if you don't dam it up. There shall be no end to the flow if you don't put it in the wrong pocket.*
>
> *If you build bags to hold it, the bags will have holes in them. You won't be any better for it. But if you make it the conduit, if you make yourself the flow in, flow out, there shall be such an exceeding flow that you will say, "How is there enough to do this, and more left over besides?" For I am still the God who multiplies. I'm still the God who takes the fishes and loaves, feeds the multitudes and sends twelve baskets full home on*

purpose. I'm the God who goes before the gleaners and leaves handfuls on purpose.

I'm the God who orders destiny. And so I call you, says the Lord, Conduit for Resources, in and out, in and out, in and out. And watch if every dream of your heart is not made manifest and answered by my flow. For my abundant provision is not for you alone. It is for others but surely shall fill you abundantly says the Lord your God, Jehovah Jireh, your Provider.

Both these words were spoken in regard to money. Both words were an exhortation to cooperate with the Father's plan. God pays His bills. He knew what was coming, and He knew what He intended to ask of us. He supplied the money up front and made it known that when it happened we were to be sure to remember *our people*.[9] It was not for us alone. His Kingdom operates on an *in and out* economy, and He makes us conduits to give and to receive. Whatever food we serve up on our banquet table, we can rest in His unchanging faithfulness to us. He supplies the seed. He supplies it abundantly. And as long as we give it out, there is no end to the supply.

the INVITATION

The Lord has put this book into your hands because He wants to take you higher. He has more for your life than what you have been living, and He has come to bring you freedom and victory. His first invitation to you came in the very beginning of the book when He dared you to believe that you, yes you, could actually fly! And to counter quote Peter Pan, "The moment you believe you can fly, you are forever able to do it." You signed up, and He began to teach you about how He wanted you to always take off from a high place. He made shambles of all your self-rejection and set your heart on fire with the amazing way that He loves you. He is crazy proud of you on every day and you began to know it. The world felt safe once again, and it was okay to remove all those coats you had piled on to protect yourself. Then, even though you had some trepidation, you began to bravely test out your own uniqueness, taking it for a spin around the block.

You checked out of the orphanage and came home to your Father's heart. Right there on His front porch you went over and crawled up on His lap, and for a long time you stayed there. You didn't say much and you didn't ask for much. Sometimes, He would just carry you with Him as He went about His work, and as time passed, you began to lift your head with curiosity, looking all about, watching all the activity that He and His kids were involved in. You would hear yourself thinking, "Umph! Well, I could do **that**!" Then suddenly you were squirming to get down. Suddenly you could feel a new future rising up inside you. It was the future

God had written for you all along, but now your eyes had opened, and now you could see it.

The Lord laughed with delight. He put you down and sent you on your way. Oh, you were so filled with His love, and all you could think about was getting your hands on that list. Yes, that is all you wanted to do. You just had to get your hands on that list … the list where you had so painstakingly recorded every wrong that every person had done to you. You knew exactly where it was, and you got it and tore it up. You even tore up the list that you kept about yourself. What freedom! Over the years, you had worn out dozens of bold, black markers keeping those lists up to date. You felt so strong now, afraid of nothing.

We have come to the end of the book. We have come to the culmination of His invitation over our lives. His invitation is a costly invitation. He knows that it is love that will put you in the driver's seat. He knows that it is love that will consistently cause your heart to be fully engaged. This chapter is the capstone and He invites you, "Will you allow Me to teach you to love with My love?"

> *It's only in this expressing of gratitude for the life we already have, do we discover the life we've always wanted …a life we can take, give thanks for, and break for others.*
>
> —STEVE SHULTZ

CONCLUSION

Some will fly. Some will come up even higher. But then there are those who will take it all the way. They will soar like eagles. They will run and not grow weary. They will walk and not faint.[10] What will you do?

my PRAYER of BLESSING OVER YOU

Father, I pray now for each one into whose hand You have placed this book. Thank You that You are going to mend and restore all that has been torn from each of their lives. Let them know that You are carrying them in Your arms. As deep as the enemy has taken them, so high shall they soar with You on eagle's wings. Thank You that You are a God Who makes all things new. Their season of struggle is over, and the road that now rises up before them is a road that will be marked by abundant increase and fruitfulness. They will tell of Your goodness to others and many will be drawn to them. Joy and laughter will be their portion, and their hunger to know You and to know Your heart will be satisfied. You will be their Teacher, and You will direct them in the way that You want them to go. Thank You, Father, that You are going to stir them up and awaken them to the dreams that

You have put in their heart … those things that are recorded in their book of life. And they shall walk in those things in days ahead. I speak Your peace and comfort over them and I ask, Lord Jesus, that You would make them bold as lions. To You, Father, Son, and Holy Spirit, be all glory forever and ever! Amen.

THOUGHTS for REFLECTION and DISCUSSION

1. Think about a situation in your life where hope has been deferred. Share your heart with the Lord concerning what you long to see happen in that situation. Trust Him with the delay, thanking Him for His hand that has been working in ways that you have not even understood. Then praise Him and declare by faith that the answer is now near.

2. Waiting is not passive. Waiting is a form of adversity, a very real test of our faith and endurance. God always makes it worth the wait! Ask the Lord to show you if there is something in your life where you have done all you know to do. Receive His affirmation that comes with knowing that. Then let go of that thing and posture your heart to wait on Him.

3. Read Luke 6:27-49.
   - What stands out to you in this passage?
   - What do you hear the Holy Spirit speaking to your heart?
   - How will you respond to that?
4. How high will you fly?
5. Imagine you have set your banquet table for others to come and eat. Imagine yourself there at the party.
   - Who is there with you?
   - What is happening?
   - What are you feeling?

Endnotes

1. Proverbs 13:12, NIV.
2. Hebrews 11:8, NIV.
3. Romans 4:18, NIV.
4. Genesis 45:5-7, NIV.
5. 1 Corinthians 2:25, NIV.
6. Matthew 23:10, NIV.
7. Hebrews 12:2, NIV.
8. Luke 6:27-49, TLB.
9. Isaiah 58:7, NIV.
10. Isaiah 40:31, NIV.

> Contentment is the peaceful happiness that comes when we are in awe of how God feels about us.
>
> —Graham Cooke

Meet the Author

Patty D. Johnson

Patty considers her greatest achievement to be learning to love. Through decades of unanswered prayers, gut-wrenching sorrow, fear, and shame as she was disowned by her parents, cursed repeatedly, and coped with sons in and out of prison, Patty turned to a life of worship and prayer. It's what saved her.

She and her husband, Hollis, have been married almost 50 years and have moved 22 times. With their four children and a chance to experience life all around the country, Patty has learned to appreciate the steady, saving, constant grace of the One who has enraptured her heart and kept her through it all.

She writes this book from a place of peace, from a place of knowing that God holds it all in the palm of His hand and that He loves her totally, completely, and unconditionally. Her unshakable faith for victory and her passion for others to know the authentic, all-powerful love of Heaven compels her to be vulnerable here, between these pages, sharing her story so you can find your own way into the driver's seat of your life!

Patty has a degree in mechanical engineering from Penn State, is an ordained minister with the Assemblies of God, and served in leadership with Aglow International for twelve years. She now lives in the beautiful Smokey Mountains of East Tennessee. She loves to speak at conferences and churches and help others learn how to live outrageously free.

Meet the Author

To learn more or to invite Patty to speak at your conference or event:

www.pattydjohnson.com

> *For I have loved you with an everlasting love; I have drawn you with unfailing kindness.*
>
> —Jeremiah 31:3, NIV

www.ingramcontent.com/pod-product-compliance
Lightning Source LLC
LaVergne TN
LVHW051601070426
835507LV00021B/2710